CHaRAcTeR ANiMaTiON CRAsh CoUrSE!

CHARACTER ANIMATION CRASH COURSE!

by **Eric Goldberg**

SILMAN-JAMES PRESS   LOS ANGELES

10 9 8 7 6 5 4 3 2 1

Library of Congress Cataloging-in-Publication Data

Goldberg, Eric.
Character animation crash course! / by Eric Goldberg.
p. cm.
ISBN 978-1-879505-97-1 (alk. paper)
1. Animated films--Technique. 2. Drawing--Technique. 3. Characters and
characteristics in art. I. Title.
NC1765.G65 2008
741.5'8--dc22
2008024765

Cover design by Eric Goldberg

Book design by William Morosi

Printed in Canada

Silman-James Press
1181 Angelo Drive
Beverly Hills, CA 90210

For Susan,

the best Art Director a guy could marry,
whose gentle cajoling, acts of persuasion,
remarkable patience, inspired cheerleading,
and any other technique, short of
physical violence or blackmail,
made it possible for you to be holding this book in your hands.

Contents

Foreword

When I first started making films, books about character animation were rare, and most were written from the distant, historical perspective of an observer.

Of the meager handful of books that actually discussed how to *do* animation, only two were really good: *Walt Disney's Tips On Animation* from the Disneyland Art Corner and the classic *Advanced Animation* by Preston Blair.

In the half century since, *many* animation books have been written, but still few are considered indispensable to people interested in doing animation themselves. To that exclusive club we must add the book you now hold in your hand: *Character Animation Crash Course*.

Among Eric's many achievements is the "Friend Like Me" sequence from Walt Disney Pictures' *Aladdin*, a chunk of pure cartoon magic so dense that it can be enjoyed two ways: at regular speed or one frame at a time… where every aspect of Eric's astonishing embellishments, caricature, and razor-sharp timing can be savored like fine wine.

In this jam-packed book and CD Eric will show you the rules for getting the most out of your animation. If you learn them well, you'll be good. If you can internalize these rules to the point where you can call upon them without thinking, you'll be exceptional.

And if you learn them as well as Eric, you might even be able to successfully break a few of these rules and add to cumulative knowledge of how to make pencil lines (or pixels, clay, stop-motion models, etc.) come to life.

You might even become accomplished enough to write the next great animation book. Good thing the rest of us don't have to wait until then.

We have this terrific book right now.

Brad Bird — Writer/Director, *The Iron Giant*, *The Incredibles*, *Ratatouille*

Introduction

How do you create an animated character that has a distinct personality? How do you get from that blank sheet of paper or empty monitor screen to something that anyone, from age 6 to 96, can recognize as a living, breathing, emoting individual? Over the years there have been many books about animation: the coffee-table tomes lavishly illustrated with glossy color stills of all your favorite cartoon stars, anecdotal reminiscences of the halcyon days of animation's Golden Age ("When Walt raised his eyebrow…"), in-depth exposés of the seamy underbelly of the corrupt and moral-destroying medium of cartoons, and scholarly dissertations on the existential impact of fantasy violence considered in a media-continuum from the Road Runner to the Powerpuff Girls. There have also been technique books, some quite informative, that break down and analyze a myriad of actions for the eager animator to utilize. But where is the book that tells you how to conceive your characters and their movements from the inside out?

It has always been my strong belief that you can't animate a character successfully until you know *who* that character is first. *Then* the technique is applied to communicate to the audience what that character is thinking and feeling. This, then, is the book I wish I had when I was first learning my craft. The first part stresses the thought and preparation required to animate, and the second part is a hands-on, no-nonsense manual describing classic animation techniques, all in service of getting great performances from your characters. On the technical side, there are some basic things not included in this book (varieties of walks and runs, classic character types, etc.) that I feel are already quite well covered in books readily available on the market. Instead, I'm trying to include the information that describes *why* actions appear a certain way, and the techniques used to create them. There are reasons why certain things look the way they do on screen, so here they are – how they work, and why they work the way they do. There will be some theory along the way, plus frequent referencing of classic cartoons for those wanting to see the ideas expressed here in glorious movement and color. Mostly, though, it's the nuts-and-bolts stuff that no one ever tells the serious student or the avid professional.

It is essentially the souped-up version of my animation notes, created in the 1980's for up-and-coming animators at my former London studio, Pizazz Pictures. These notes have been Xeroxed and copied (and, yes, plagiarized) for a couple of decades now, passed from animator to animator as a kind of underground secret source of information. Well, now you hold it in your hands, complete with updated material, new chapters, new drawings (clearer ones, I hope, and ones the major studios won't consider copyright infringement), and further enhancements added during my years at Walt Disney Feature Animation.

I've had the benefit of working with some fantastic animators in my formative years, especially Richard Williams, Ken Harris, Art Babbitt, and Tissa David, whose knowledge (and generosity with it) continues to fuel and inspire me. I've also spent many years analyzing and dissecting the work of all of my animation heroes, attempting to distill their awesome mastery of the medium into the miracle elixir, "Essence of Cartoon." I have derived so much pleasure and creative fulfillment from these people and their craft that I hope this book honors their tradition of imparting their wisdom to those who seek to know more.

I'm particularly concentrating on traditional cartoon animation, since it's what animators most closely associate with my technique. However, applying these ideas to more subtle, realistic animation can often be simply a matter of toning down the broadness but utilizing the same principles – and, of course, these principles are just as viable in the ever-expanding fields of computer, Flash, and paperless animation as they are in the old-school hand-drawn world.

In the end, no one can really "teach" anyone how to animate, and I make no attempt to do so here. The best I can do is offer insights and methods that have helped me over the years. The rest is up to the individual – to harness the information into something usable for his or her own creative expression. Whatever twists, turns, and technologies continue to develop in our medium, the investment of personal feelings and emotions will always be animation's future.

And now some set-up: two characters you will be seeing frequently on these pages are:

Norman   and   Earless Dog.

They have both served me well over the years, as they're easy to draw and very malleable, so they're perfect ambassadors for the cartoony stuff I'm setting forth here. However, don't be fooled by their inherent elasticity: the same principles laid out here apply to even the most constructed and anatomical of characters.

The other unique feature to point out is that several of the principles in this book have been fully animated and stored as movie files on the enclosed CD, complete with drawing numbers, indications of keys and breakdowns, and inbetween charts. If a picture is worth a thousand words, then moving pictures must be worth 24 times that, at least. They can be accessed one at a time as reference, or, if you're game enough, you can read the book next to your laptop, and play the movie as the examples come up. Within the text, each illustration that has an accompanying movie will be indicated by a symbol and number in the margin:

SP 6

Happy animating!

Special Thanks

It turns out that creating an animation book is as collaborative a process as animation itself. Herewith, a deferential nod and a raised glass of pencil shavings to those who helped me make this a reality and not a pipe dream:

— The nice people at Silman–James Press, Tom Rusch, Tom Morr, and especially the unbelievably patient and encouraging Gwen Feldman, who allowed my work schedule to trample over my deadlines, but never wavered in her support to make the book I really wanted.

— Stuart and Amy Ng, who hooked me up with the nice people at Silman-James Press in the first place, and who continue to be great cheerleaders for animation.

— William Morosi, the fabulous (and animation-knowledgeable) designer of this book's layout, and a swell fellow with whom to chew the animation fat as well.

— My esteemed animation colleagues Brad Bird, Ron Clements, Andreas Deja, Roy E. Disney, Don Hahn, John Lasseter, John Musker, David Silverman, and Charles Solomon, for lending their time and expertise in support of this project.

— Amy Ellenwood, Monica Elsbury, Cassandra Anderson, Karen Paik, and Heather Feng for helping to wrangle the above esteemed animation colleagues.

— Kent Gordon of Disney Animation, who showed me, the world's most un-tech person, the key to making high-quality animation movie files with no image degradation, Scott Lowe, who mastered the disc material beautifully (and quickly!), and Chris Lovejoy, who had the awesome task of duplicating all of them.

— Caroline Cruikshank, Theresa Wiseman, and Jon Hooper for providing their copies of my original notes when I had gaps in my own collection.

— Mark Pudleiner, Jennifer Cardon Klein, Kira Lehtomaki, Bobby Beck of Animation Mentor, and Alex Williams, for their vigilant and successful efforts to keep bootleg copies of this book off the Internet, and to those who graciously removed them from their sites.

— Bert Klein, Scott Johnston, Tom and Pat Sito, Sue and Bill Kroyer, Bob Kurtz and Theresa Uchi, Phil Pignotti, Tom Roth, Hyun-min Lee, Tina Price of Creative Talent Network, and the extended network of animation friends and colleagues over the years, whose advice and reassurance, especially during the bad times, are always appreciated.

— From The Walt Disney Company, Howard Green, Margaret Adamic, Dave Bossert, Eddie Khanbeigi, Christine Chrisman, and Katie Schock for allowing me generous and liberal use of the Genie, Aladdin, Phil, the Snotty Six flamingos, and an actual frame from *Peter Pan*, to demonstrate animation principles.

— From Walt Disney Animation Studios, Tenny Chonin, Dawn Rivera-Ernster, and Pat Beckman, whose support and encouragement not just for this project but also for the ongoing mentorship and education of young animators at the studio is an inspiration.

— Last but by no means least, my wife Susan and daughters Jenny and Rachel, who for all these years happily and unquestioningly accepted that I would occasionally burst out singing "Goodnight, Sweet Dreams" in Bugs Bunny's voice or make involuntary Donald Duck quacks whenever I dropped something. Now that's love.

Definition of Terms

Like the instruction manuals that scream at us, "Read me first," I recommend a perusal of these terms before diving into the nitty-gritty of the text. Many of the terms may already be familiar to you; some may have my own personal twist. In any event, knowing this stuff will just make going through the book easier, since it is written for the most part without stopping to define terms every two sentences.

Accents — The parts of the soundtrack that are louder or more stressed, which should be indicated in the animation. In dialogue, it can be louder parts of words or words that carry emotional stress; in music, it can be major beats or particularly present instruments.

Anticipation — The smaller preparatory action that precedes a major action, used to show that a character must physically prepare to perform an action or gesture.

Attitude Pose — A pose that expresses, through the entire body, what a character is thinking and feeling.

Attitude Walk — A walk that expresses, both through poses and movement, how a character feels.

Background — The painted (usually) scene against which the full-color characters perform in a finished scene. ("BG" for short.)

Breakdown — The initial drawing or position made between two keys, which defines how a character transitions from one idea to the next. ("BD" for short.)

Boil — The slang term used for the evident flickering of drawings when a scene is run at speed, which results when lines and forms have not been drawn carefully enough to follow through from one drawing to the next.

Cel – Short for celluloid, the flammable material on which animation drawings were inked and painted. Replaced in later years by non-fire-hazardous acetate, the term is still in common usage (as in "held cel"), although almost all hand-drawn animation is now digitally inked and painted.

Clean-Ups – The drawings in an animation scene that are refined for final inking or scanning, usually made by placing a new sheet of paper over the rough and perfecting both the linework and the character nuances. In traditional animation today, these are the drawings the audience sees on the screen.

Cushion-Out and **Cushion-In** – The drawings that accelerate out of a pose, spaced progressively farther apart (so the action does not start abruptly), and decelerate into the following pose, spaced progressively closer together (to complete the action with a smooth settling-in). Also known as "Slow-Out and Slow-In."

Drag – The drawing of action that indicates a portion of a character lagging behind, used to create more fluidity in the perceived movement.

Eccentric Action – Specialized movement within an action that cannot be articulated through normal inbetweening. This can include leg positions in a walk or run, mouth positions, hand gestures, and elaborate movement on the entire body.

Exposure Sheet – The bible of a scene in hand-drawn animation, showing the timing, the dialogue frame-by-frame, camera and fielding information, the number of cel levels required, and how many frames each drawing should be exposed. ("X-sheet" for short.)

Extreme – A key drawing or pose that is the most exaggerated or dynamic point of a particular action.

Favoring – Making an inbetween position that favors either the position directly before it or after it, instead of making it directly in the center.

Foot – Unit by which 35mm film is measured and exposure sheets are subdivided. 1 foot = 16 frames, thus 1½ feet = 24 frames, or 1 second of screen time. There are 90 feet of film per minute of screen time.

Film Grammar – The language of filmmaking, comprised of different types of shots, staging and editing principles, and scene transitions, and how they are used by filmmakers to help tell a story.

Follow-Through — The natural elaboration of an action that shows how one part leads organically to the next until the action is resolved.

Frame — One single picture, usually equaling $\frac{1}{24}$ of a second in the cinema, whether film or digital projection is used. 24 frames = 1 second of screen time; 16 frames = 1 foot. Because of differing electrical systems around the globe, some altered frame rates occur on television broadcasts. U.S. NTSC television runs at 60 Hz per second, so some animation is timed to 30 frames per second (fps), although most is still produced at 24 fps and converted electronically. The PAL system in Europe is based on a 50Hz per second cycle, so animation is timed for 25 fps.

Held Cel — Portion of a character that is not moving and is drawn onto its own cel level, used to avoid redrawing the non-moving part over a series of frames.

Inbetween — A drawing or position made in a scene that comes between the keys and breakdowns. At times they can be right in the middle; at other times they can favor either the earlier or the later position.

Inbetween Chart — Chart on a key drawing that indicates both the spacing of the inbetweens and the order in which they are to be drawn up until the next key.

Keys — The important drawings or poses in a scene that establish the basic tent-poles of the movement and performance.

Layout — The setting in which the animated action takes place, indicating sizes of characters in relation to their background, perspective, camera position and movement, major positions of characters within the scene, lighting, and composition of the shot.

Limited Animation — Animation with a reduced number of drawings for either stylistic or economic reasons, most commonly seen in television cartoons.

Line of Action — The first line indicated in a pose, showing the basic overall posture, prior to adding the rest of the details.

Lip-Sync — The animation of lip and mouth shapes in synchronization to the number of frames indicated for each dialogue sound on the exposure sheets.

Mass — A character's personal dimensionality; what his shapes look like in three dimensions, moving around.

Moving Hold — A minimal amount of movement used to keep a character alive while still communicating a strong pose or attitude. Also known as a "Glorified Pose."

Ones – The exposure of drawings or positions for one frame each; there would be 24 drawings on ones for a second of screen time.

Overlap – The actions that indicate that not all parts of a character arrive at the same time, and can go past the point of arrival and settle back. Used to indicate weight, movement of clothing, hair, etc.

Pantomime – An animation scene that has no dialogue, in which a character's thoughts and emotions are expressed entirely through his poses, expressions, and movement.

Partial – A rough animation drawing that only includes the eccentric actions (lip-sync, leg positions, a shut or partially shut eye), leaving the remainder to be done as a straight inbetween (usually by an assistant animator or rough inbetweener).

Passing Position – In a walk, the intermediate pose in which one leg is passing in front of the other.

Phrasing – The process of containing a sentence of dialogue within an organic pattern of movement.

Pose-to-Pose – The method of animating by establishing key poses first, and then going back in to complete the breakdowns and inbetweens.

Recoil – The after-effect of an abrupt stop, where a character (or parts of him) go past the eventual final pose and settle back into it.

Roughs – The drawings in an animation scene made prior to clean-up, usually associated with the animator's first pass of realizing the movement and performance.

Secondary Action – Action animated in addition to a major action, used to show nuance within the main idea. For example, a major action could be a character settling into an impatient pose; the secondary action could be the character tapping his foot impatiently to a faster rhythm.

Silhouette – The overall shape of a pose, which should read clearly even when the pose is blacked in without its internal details.

Spacing – The process of determining how far apart the positions should be from one another, based on the knowledge that the farther apart, the faster the action, the closer together, the slower the action.

Stagger – The mechanical manipulation of frames to achieve a vibration on screen.

Staggered Timing – Parts of a scene or piece of animation that do not occur at the same time. For example, several characters doing the same dance step could be on staggered timing (one frame earlier, two frames later, etc.) in order for the group action to appear more naturally on the screen.

Staging – The positioning of characters in a scene for maximum emotional content and clear readability of actions.

Storytelling Drawings – The drawings in a scene that succinctly communicate to an audience the important ideas expressed through the action.

Straight-Ahead – The technique of animating in order, from the beginning to the end of a scene, to achieve a natural flow from one drawing to the next. Not as easily controlled as the pose-to-pose method, straight-ahead animation requires strict attention to the maintaining of volumes and sizes, but can result in very fluid-looking movement.

Strobing – The unwanted effect of a vibration across the screen, usually associated with vertical shapes perpendicular to the horizon. Strobing would occur if a character were animated on twos while the camera panned on ones – almost the optical version of a "stagger." The way to fix this problem is to put in the single inbetweens on ones for the duration of the pan.

Successive Breaking of Joints – The term first coined by animator Art Babbitt to describe how a character can move fluidly based on anatomy. You can show a "wave" action in a character's arm, for example, by having the arm travel downward, "breaking" at the elbow, and then successively "breaking" at the wrist as the rest of the arm catches up, and then breaking in the opposite direction at elbow and wrist on the way back up.

Texture – The appearance of differences in timing, spacing, pacing, and emotional range within an animation scene, in order to keep the scene interesting and believable to an audience.

Thumbnails – A series of quick sketches (usually small, thus "thumbnail") used to figure out major poses and storytelling drawings in a scene.

Tie-Downs – The drawings made as a secondary stage in rough animation that further refine the expressions and details throughout a scene, usually made by an animator on top of his own initial roughs.

Timing – The process of determining how long each drawing or position should be on screen, based on the knowledge that 24 frames equal one second of screen time.

Twos – The exposure of drawings or positions for two frames apiece; there would be twelve drawings on twos for one second of screen time.

Traceback – Portion of a character that is held for several frames, but "traced back" to an original source drawing over the remaining amount of the hold. This is used to keep a character feeling alive, rather than separating the held portion onto a separate level.

Volume – The amount of space a character takes up; even if a character is squashed, stretched, or distorted, his volume should remain consistent.

Weight – Indication of a character's poundage, shown through the timing, overlap, and style of movement.

CONCEPTION

Attitude Poses

Attitude poses are those succinct drawings in your scene that convey what your character is feeling while he's moving. If you can develop the ability to encapsulate an expression or attitude in a single drawing, then you've already gone some distance toward successfully communicating to your audience. By using strong attitudes, you can animate into, out of, or around, them — thus making your animation more dynamic and more readable. They also define who your characters are by the specific way they are posed for their particular personalities. One of my favorite examples of this is from Tex Avery's *Little Rural Riding Hood*. Upon entering the nightclub, City Wolf walks in, nose high in the air, his concave back leading in a supple way down the back of his smoothly dragging legs. His hand grips that of Country Wolf, a flailing compendium of disjointed angles and frenetic movement that define him as…well, an idiot. Classic stuff.

When you start working, imagine yourself as a comic strip artist: the great ones all had the ability to express action and emotion in a single drawing. (Charles Schulz, Walt Kelly, Bill Watterson, and Johnny Hart immediately spring to mind.)

Below are some poses that have an imaginary "line of action" running through them. This gives your poses thrust and purpose – in a way, it's like developing the line of your character's spine, and then building the figure on top.

The strength of your poses can also be tested by how well they read in silhouette:

When approaching a scene, make a series of drawings that "tell the story" of the scene (how the character feels, where he's going, what occurs physically in the plot, the character's attitudes throughout) in order of their appearance in the scene. Don't even worry about timing at this stage; just make the drawings communicate. In the case of television or commercial productions, these will often be the drawings you would get from the director as pose/layout drawings (an extension of the way Golden Age shorts directors worked). Whether they are provided for you, or you create them yourself, these storytelling drawings aren't necessarily the most extreme drawings in the scene. Rather, they are the ones most comfortable for the eye to settle on (while still retaining strength and directness in drawing). These drawings can be telegraphed strongly for more extreme, stylized action (Chuck Jones' *Dover Boys*, or your average Avery cartoon) or animated into and out of more subtly for feature-style animation (which covers the poses with more secondary actions, overlap, limbs on different timings, etc. Milt Kahl was a firm advocate of storytelling drawings).

I sometimes call this the "Name That Tune" school of animating. For those of you not ancient enough to remember this TV game show, contestants competed to name the title of a song in the fewest number of notes. ("I can name that tune in three notes, Bill.") If you can "name that scene" in the fewest number of drawings, your scene will convey a great deal of clarity to the viewer.

Here's a sequence of five storytelling drawings, each of which represents a different attitude:

Here's what the character is thinking in each:

1. "Hey, I'm a pretty slick item, as I rear up to start running."
2. "Here I go, doop-de-doo, a goofball without a care in the world."
3. "Whoops! Almost mashed a daisy!"
4. "I'll be real careful so as not to step on the delicate little thing."
5. "!@#%&*@!!"

Note that we're not just talking facial expressions here; the *entire body* is used as a visual indicator to the thought process.

Attitude Poses in Walks and Runs

Showing attitudes in walks and runs is a vital tool for communicating. Instead of just getting the character from one place to the next, use the journey to tell your audience how he's feeling. Here are just a few examples:

STEALTH

TREPIDATION

ANGRY DETERMINATION

MISCHIEF

SYCOPHANTIC
(SHUFFLING BACKWARDS)

A live-action walk actually spends more screen time in the "passing position," where one leg passes in front of the other, but an attitude walk reverses this, spending more screen time around the poses where the foot first contacts the ground. Although this is technically "incorrect," if you spend fewer frames on the passing position, and more frames cushioning into and out of the attitudes, it shows your audience the "intent" of the walk.

Here's a step-by-step method for animating an attitude walk:

AP 1

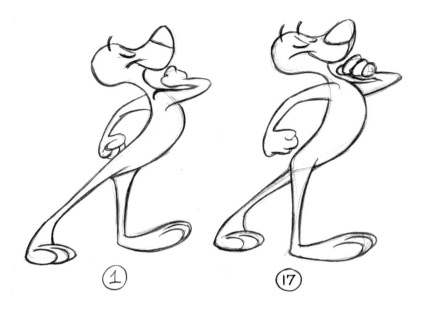

Step 1: Determine a pose that expresses the feeling your character needs for the scene (in this case, a proud, confident strut). Call it **①**.

Step 2: Develop the same pose for the opposite arms and legs, bearing in mind angle changes, weight shifts, and foreshortening. Call it **⑰**. This means our doggie will take a step every 16 frames.

Step 3: Develop two "passing position" breakdowns, **9** between ① and ⑰, and **25** between ⑰ and ①, making a 32-frame cycle. In a strut such as this, the passing position is better as a "down" (instead of an "up" for a normal walk) because it emphasizes the slide up into the exaggerated, chest-out pride. Also note that opposite things happen on the breakdown: head down instead of up, back convex instead of concave, wrists "broken" in the opposite direction as the arms move through.

When charted as above, the spacing is much wider through the passing position, and more cushioned toward the keys ① and ⑰, meaning you'll read his "attitude" much more strongly, because more screen time is being spent around the idea poses.

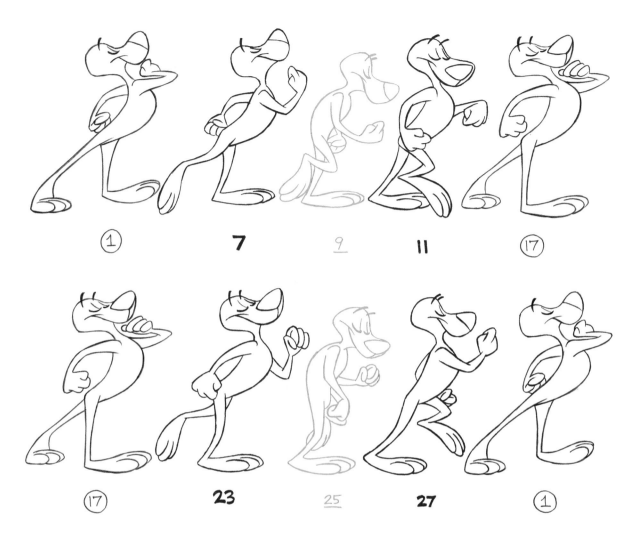

Step 4: Now go in and further break down the action, putting 7 between ① and **9**, 11 between **9** and ⑰, 23 between ⑰ and **25**, and 27 between **25** and ①. Note, however, that these drawings are made to further enhance and favor keys ① and ⑰: 7 is closer to ① than **9**, 11 is closer to ⑰ than **9**, 23 is closer to ⑰ than **25**, and 27 is closer to ① than **25**. The only place this favoring does not occur is when the foot contacts the ground, since this is a center-screen walk cycle. (This means that the contact foot must be animated in such a way that its spacing appears even, since a constantly panning background will be going across the screen at the same rate. If the foot is favored during contact, it will appear to slip and slide during the constant rate pan.) Now that you have these drawings, it is a simple matter to fill in the remaining inbetweens as charted, following arcs as the drawings indicate.

Moving Holds

Lots of animators use this technique to make a pose read, but still give the character some life. The majority of the character can be traced back or on a held cel, with one or two moving bits (eyes, ears, whiskers, or some sort of secondary foot or hand movement). Another moving hold technique is to have the character cushion in slowly to your storytelling pose for what would be the duration of the proposed hold. (For example, if your character is meant to be held for 24 frames, draw one key slightly less progressed to the final pose, and do tight inbetweens that cushion in to the last key over the 24-frame length.) Computer animation makes even more frequent use of moving holds, since the common experience has been that having a CG character in a frozen hold makes it look like a very dead plastic model.

Example #1: Hipster wolf, looking bored and cool. His body is on a held cel, and the only action is the coin being flipped repeatedly, and the wafting of the non-PC cigarette smoke.

Example #2: Peeved pig registers disgruntlement: 1. Eyes flick toward camera. 2. One eyebrow raises up. 3. One ear flaps down. Each action is timed separately instead of all at once, to make each minimal move more pointed.

Attitude Poses in an Acting or Dialogue Scene

Here are some ways that strong attitudes enhance a variety of animation scenes:

In a pantomime scene, poses can be telegraphed for comic effect (with good elaboration on the animation and overlap whenever necessary). Very few inbetweens are needed between major poses. A fine example: Mike Lah's "baseball" scene from Avery's *The Chump Champ*.

In a dialogue or monologue, poses can also be utilized the same way for exaggeration and stylization. Check out Ken Harris' Charlie Dog "Da city!" speech from Jones' *Often an Orphan*.

In a musical scene, a major pose per musical phrase gives the animation direction and humor. Two examples, one animated, one live-action: 1. Ward Kimball's beautifully stylized animation of the title song in Disney's *The Three Caballeros*. 2. Gene Kelly, Frank Sinatra, and Jules Munshin singing "New York, New York" in *On the Town* ("The Bronx is up, and the Battery's down!").

Animating in this way gives your characters force of intent. Obviously, not all animation can be thought of in this manner, but how subtly or broadly you handle it can have a bearing on an infinite number of situations. If handled broadly, the animation is stylized, telegraphing the audience — first one thought is read, then the next, then the next, and so on. If handled more subtly, which usually requires the less-frenetic pacing found in features, it can result in more realistic movement but still give strength and intent to a scene. Milt Kahl's Shere Khan or Glen Keane's Tarzan are sterling examples of animation that uses great storytelling drawings.

Attitude Poses Developed from an Outside Source

When you are called upon to animate an already-established, distinctive style, as is frequently the case in television commercials, look at the source material and find out how the artist handles various attitudes and postures you may need. Whether you're animating a famous comic-strip character, Japanese woodcuts, or fashion illustration, each would have attitudes that the original artist utilizes to communicate in the printed form. Examine how the artist expresses joy, sorrow, anger, relaxation, dejection; how the figure walks, runs, rests — the characteristic poses that make this artwork unique. Then utilize these as the storytelling drawings or action keys to give your animation accuracy to the original (and allow your audience to recognize the original). Just for yocks, imagine you got the secret dream assignment of many animators: do a 30-second test of Bill Watterson's *Calvin and Hobbes*. If you can figure out a better place to get your poses than in Watterson's beautiful, practically animated-already drawings, then good luck to you.

Limited Animation

Attitude poses can be even more important in TV cartoons, since they rarely have the budgets and schedules for niceties like overlap and slow cushions. While it's true that much of television animation rests on the quality of the writing and voice work, the best examples utilize the visual as well as the verbal. John Kricfalusi's *Ren & Stimpy* is one of the best modern usages of strong posing for limited animation; also check out the wonderful UPA cartoons to see how it was done by the masters, especially John Hubley's *Rooty Toot Toot* and Bobe Cannon's *Gerald McBoing-Boing.*

A Word about Thumbnails

I'm sad to report that I very rarely use thumbnail sketches to help determine my poses, since I prefer to work full-size. For me, this is the most comfortable method, because I can better explore using the entire body to be expressive. However, there are many staunch supporters of the thumbnail, some world-class animators among them, so who am I to disagree? If you find them useful, go for it.

2

Acting in Animation – Part 1: Getting Started

What Is "Good Acting" in Animation?

Simply, "good acting" is that which convinces an audience that the character exists. He should look as if *he* is in control, not a pile of drawings pushed around by an unseen artist. If he is *re*acting to stimulus, physical or emotional, he should be animated in a way that tells an audience that it is *he* who is reacting (*his* particular personality and facial expressions and *his* ground rules of weight and mass) and not another character. Or *hers*.

■ Get inside your characters!

They won't be alive unless *you* invest them with a personal, intuitive set of feelings. If the character is doing something physical, feel out the action for yourself (or act it out even!). Recall similar incidents you have experienced to that which your characters must undergo. Don't just settle for cornball clichés found in cartoons – base your drawings on a knowledge of cartooning and caricature, but also on observation of people around you and an awareness of personal experience. I'm going to concentrate primarily on pantomime here, but as you read farther, you will see that some fundamentals rely on the consideration of dialogue and plot content, even at the earliest point of character conception.

How Do You Develop a Convincing Character in Animation?

■ **Believe he exists!** No one will believe in your character unless you do first. And if this character exists, he will have certain properties, physical and emotional, that you will need to convey to an audience.

■ **Know who he is.** Any character has to be conceived from the inside out. By understanding *who* your character is, you will define movements, gestures, and behavior that reflect his outlook. Often, animation characters start with archetypes, so the audience can "get" who they are quickly. I call this the "John and Ron" technique, since John Musker and Ron Clements are the directing team that uses this method so effectively. (Heck, they darn near invented it!) Let's use Disney's *Hercules* as an example: Meg is the "tough gal with a heart of gold," Phil is the "feisty coach," a has-been with a gruff exterior. However, these characters become richer when you define for the audience *why* they have become these archetypes and how they deal with it. Meg has been hurt in love before — so much that she's developed that hard shell as a defense mechanism — and it's the prospect of true love that makes her crack. Phil is a washout, a failure: he's given up and lives a life of debauchery to help him forget — but the prospect of Herc just possibly being "the one" makes him drop his guard one more time. Now all of this may sound lofty for a broad cartoon comedy such as *Hercules*, but I assure you it is indeed the process the directors and animators went through to realize their characters. By giving your characters a history, your animation can evolve over the course of a film: start by showing the audience the archetype, and deepen it — contrast with it — when revealing the character's motives, changing attitudes, and internal conflicts.

■ **Ask yourself the right questions.** Grill yourself over all the aspects of your character until you know the answers:

• What makes your character *who* he is? What excites him? What makes him mad? What is his driving motivation? How does he look at life? What are his basic attitudes? How can you expand these basic attitudes to acquire more depth? What makes your particular character tick? What makes him unique? How do you show him thinking, changing mood?

- How does he walk? Run? Rest? How can you show what he is thinking and feeling through his movements? (Sir Laurence Olivier said that when he was realizing a character, the first thing he would crack was the character's walk.)
- How does your character interact with the other characters in the show? How does he compare and contrast with them? What properties of movement make your character unique to the others around him? In *Song of the South*, Brer Bear is big, heavy, and stupid, and his movements are correspondingly slow and ponderous. Brer Fox is cunning, excitable, talkative — and his movements are quick and slick.
- How *old* is your character? What is his weight and mass, and how does that affect his movement? How physically fit is your character? How weak?

OLD?   WEIGHTY?   FIT?   WEAK...?

- Is your character consistent? Sometimes animators can be trying so hard to express emotions that they can lose the *essence* of their particular character. Make sure your actions are consistent with his *particular* viewpoint on life.

- What are the psychological ground rules for your character that you should never, ever break? When should you break them? In other words, your character may remain consistent through most of the film, but break from his established character traits to express a different or deeper aspect of his personality. In Phil's case, he was always shown as a hot-tempered guy with a low boiling point. However, to show when Phil was truly hurt and angry, we made the choice to shrink him down into a more contained performance. By portraying him as loud and bombastic most of the time, it made a great contrast to have him quiet and restrained for his deepest emotions.

- How does your character act in repose as well as in activity? How does he react as a secondary character when another character is performing or talking?

- Can you use posture to convey emotions? How does the character's line of action/spine help to express what he's thinking and feeling? Get off the vertical when doing humans! By that, I mean there is a tendency when animating humans in a scene together to have all of them standing up straight like they have poles up their… well anyway, what's to stop you from using a variety of postures and angles within the characters to express their differences and enhance the staging?

GET OFF THE VERTICAL! Here's a dull scene in which everyone stands up perfectly straight…. Ho hum….

In this scene, Mean Lady leans forward, making her more threatening. Husband throws his chest out and leans forward on the opposite diagonal, making him more defiant. Wife curls around behind Husband, making her appear more fearful.

- Does your character adopt an attitude throughout a scene or a series of them? Is he cocky, authoritative, meek, oily, insincere, warm, indignant, recalcitrant, caring, mischievous? Does he feign sincerity when talking to another character and reveal his true nature when that character's back is turned? (Think Zero Mostel in *The Producers*.) Is your character the type to conspire with the audience and look into the camera? How do you show these attitudes and expressions succinctly? The great mime Marcel Marceau used to appear on Johnny Carson's *Tonight Show* in the 70's. Johnny once asked him how he got his performances and characters to look so realistic. His answer: what the audience sees is completely stylized, edited so that the extraneous movements are not included. If he really did something realistic, the audience wouldn't understand it!

- What is it about your character's attitudes that are unique to him? (Instead of utilizing poses that are standard animation clichés, what can you do to make poses that are unique to *this* character?)

- What value can be gained from walks and runs — speed, gait, posture — that can show the character's attitudes? In other words, it's not just enough to develop a walk. What does that walk say about how he's feeling *at the moment*?

When animating:

- Is your scene well-paced for its emotional content? Does it need to be slow, ponderous? Quick and snappy? Is there texture to the variety of timings and moods? Are your expressive poses on screen long enough to communicate to an audience?

- How does your character break out of one thought before expressing another? Are anticipations used effectively to change mood or expression?

- If there is more than one character in the scene, are their personalities clearly defined? Do you give them enough room to breathe and space to act without the audience feeling like they're watching a ping-pong match, with two characters constantly upstaging each other?

- Is your character reacting to stimulus or trying to perform a task? Is he under physical strain or unfettered? Can he perform nonchalantly? Is he interested in what he's doing, or bored, distracted?

REACTING TO STIMULUS or PERFORMING A TASK?   UNDER PHYSICAL STRAIN or UNFETTERED?

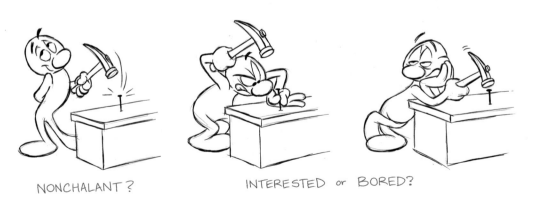

NONCHALANT?   INTERESTED or BORED?

ACTION	DIAL		
STEP ✕		1	
		3	
		5	
		7	
STEP ✕		9	
		11	
		13	
		15	
STEP ✕		17	
		19	
		21	
		23	
STOP ✕		25	
		27	
		29	
CUSHION		31	
RECOIL		33	
		35	
		37	
SETTLE		39	
		41	
		43	
HOLD		45	
		47	
		49	
		51	
		53	
		55	

- What value can be gained by restricted movement or a glorified pose? (If you want to see an expression change, don't draw attention away from it with extraneous body movements.)
- Is your character entertaining to watch? He may be expressive, and doing all the things he needs to do in the screen time, but will an audience find it interesting? Will somebody who isn't an animator be pleased to watch your creation? (Ollie Johnston: Would anyone other than your mother want to watch this scene?)

■ **Juggle the timing!** (a Dick Williams® phrase) This also applies to dialogue, but it's even more important in pantomime. If the character is doing something physical, see if he can establish a rhythm to his action – then something can happen to alter the rhythm: he gets tired, it gets slower. He gets good at it (or maybe confused), it gets quicker. *Or* something can happen to upset the rhythm completely. *Or* he can start a secondary action (looking in the other direction, trying to keep up with something) while trying to maintain his established rhythm. You can juggle timings when a character performs a repetitive function (long, short, long, short, short, long, short, long) such as typing, dialing a phone, using a calculator. If your X-sheets aren't pre-timed by the director, pre-time them yourself!

It's a perfect visual indication of the rhythms and different timings you can have in a scene before you even start drawing.

■ Believability vs. Realism

The most important attribute your character can possess is that he exists on his own terms: that his actions are a result of his thought processes, and that he has a consistent weight and volume in space (and that these things are accepted by an audience without question so that they can concentrate more on his expressions and performance). His lip-sync and accents come from his personality and are believable for his character. (Chuck Jones: "Bugs' walk isn't realistic, but it's believable.") It's not about aping realism — it's about observation and caricature, utilized in such a way that it convinces an audience of your character's existence. It could be nobody else but *that* character.

■ Think in pantomime.

A pantomime scene is automatically more difficult than a dialogue scene: A good soundtrack can very often carry lukewarm animation, and still convey humor or emotional content. ("Rocky and Bullwinkle" never had the time or budget for lavish animation; in fact, they cheaped it out. However, they spent their dollars wisely on great scripts and great voice talent.) Pantomime has no crutches — it is the animator, center stage, alone! If the scene works without sound in conveying emotions and physical properties, that's the acid test. (Jones: If the scene works without sound, it's animation. If you can tell what's going on without picture, it's radio.) Moreover, the types of things included in a good pantomime scene (strong attitude poses, good timing, establishing and breaking rhythms, change of attitude) are also the same types of things that should be in a good dialogue scene.

■ **Use the entire body to express what your character is feeling.**

Don't just concentrate on the face and upper torso to tell the audience what's going through your character's mind. The entire body – through expressive attitude poses, and through the type and quality of the body's movements – should support what is going on in the character's head, and make strong statements about who he is.

Examples: Glen Keane's *Tarzan* – A human, caught between animal and human behavior. His postures and movements show how comfortable he is on the animal side – he walks on his knuckles and picks up fruit with his foot, like an ape. When he fights Sabor, his animal instincts show through as quickness and agility – the actions and reactions are those of an animal in conflict.

Chuck Jones' Bugs and Daffy – Bugs has confident, relaxed movements that show he is always in control. His casual walk says that nothing fazes him. Daffy has a cowardly, "Get-the-hell-out-of-there" sneak. His craven movements are contrasted with his overzealous screaming and humiliating attempts to make Bugs a fall guy.

"Phil" in *Hercules* is part goat, so many of his movements and gestures are goat-like – he eats clay bowls, he paws the ground, he head-butts, he gives forth with involuntary "baa-aa-ahs."

■ How do you make a character sincere?

A lot of the sincerity comes from what has just been described. However, the character is not meant to work in a vacuum – he must relate to all the characters with whom he comes in contact. It is these relationships that often reflect sincerity the most – how your character regards the other characters in the show. If your character shows care and concern for the ones he bonds with closely in the show, that's a tangible form of sincerity. If he actively hates the villain, and you show that through his actions and expressions, that's sincerity, too. It's all part of the larger picture of not only believing that your character exists, but that he exists in a world with rules and history, populated by other characters who interact with his story and goals. And speaking of goals – that's a good quality for any character, whether it's a negative goal (taking over the world) or a positive goal (yearning to be free). Giving your character a goal (a "want," in Disney parlance), and keeping it in mind as you animate, colors everything the character will do – you can portray him as "incomplete" before he accomplishes it, and "whole" when he does.

■ Showing a range of emotions:

Even when you have strong psychological ground rules for a character, you must show a breadth and depth to the range of emotions for the character to ring true. If a character is generally grouchy, that doesn't mean you animate him like a grouch in every scene – something must make him laugh, even if it's a hardened sense of cynicism. Something must crack that grouchy shell and make him *feel,* even if it's against everything he believes in (especially!!). Something must excite him to passion – even if it's the flame of a desire re-kindled from a long time ago. (See why a history is important?) The important thing to remember is that the range of emotions you show must be true to who that character is. Pocahontas is a free spirit with a love for her people and their regard for nature. If she smiles, it's with the excitement of new possibilities, or her contentment with the natural world, but *never* out of sarcasm or a sense of irony (like Phil, for example). If she gets angry, it's because of pride for her people, not because she's petulant and not getting her way. The choices you make for the range are all filtered through who that character is.

■ "Rhapsody in Blue" – A case history

I've given a lot of complex information here, so as a way of boiling it down into something more easily gettable, let's concentrate on "Rhapsody in Blue" from *Fantasia/2000*. Here's what I knew about my characters *before* we started animating. Some of this came out in the storyboarding process; a lot of it came from knowing who the players were and what their desires were.

John — Heading toward old age, torn between who he wants to be (a fun-loving guy, acting like a kid) and who he is forced to be (a sober, stuffy, dignified member of society). His wife Margaret glares him down when he tries to have fun, so his movements are a continual contrast — broad, energetic (well, as energetic as he can be given his weight) when acting out his fantasies, contrasted with moody resignation when hauled back to reality.

Joe — Middle-aged, Joe is the symbol of the Depression. He's jobless, with absolutely no hope of finding employment in the current climate. He has a slow, "It's an effort just to put one foot in front of the other," walk, staring straight ahead with a mixture of despair and futility. Joe is also torn with moral dilemmas — he can't pay, he's hungry, so what does he do when faced with temptation? He takes the realist's view of survival first, but not without some soul-searching.

Rachel — Based on our own daughter (albeit when she was quite young). She's privileged (not based on our bank accounts), but she's not happy. She's actually quite overwhelmed by the world, her tiny stature hardly a match for the whirling expectations demanded of her in New York "enhancement" classes. Her movements suggest those of a little girl for whom everything is too big or too complex, and she can't control her awkward little body without something going awry.

Duke — The embodiment of jazz. His love for jazz shows in his body movements and gestures — he's spontaneous, improvisational, dynamic, inventive, cool. When he's in the groove, his movements are smooth and slick — like it was meant to be. As it is, Duke is the most important character in the show, because it is his spontaneous choice for his own life that is the catalyst for everyone else finding their dreams.

Knowing who these characters are, I also knew what they wanted. The visualization of their goals became the centerpiece of the show, with all of them ice skating at Rockefeller Center, looking their elegant best.

Rachel just wants to spend time with her parents. So her movements are joyous and confident when skating with them. (They'd never drop her!)

Joe just wants a job, money to live, a clean shirt. His movements are elegant — it's the first time he hasn't felt like a slob in years.

Duke wants to play jazz. His movements while skating and drumming are smooth, effortless, sensual, cool. It's where he really feels comfortable — at home.

John wants to be free. Free of constraints, free of Margaret, free of everything that's expected of him — so he takes flight, literally. It takes a bit to hoist his bulk off the ground, but he doesn't care. He's free as a bird.

So now if you're at all inspired to pop in the DVD for a peek, bear in mind that this was all the stuff we knew *before* anything was animated.

Recommended Cartoons:

The Little Whirlwind (Mickey Mouse/Disney) — Clear poses, good timing and elaboration, attitude changes, value from walks, mostly by master Fred Moore. Acting with posture (whirlwind).

The Bird Came C.O.D. (Conrad Cat/WB) — Defining a character through movement, timing, gesture, posing (mostly Ken Harris).

Bear Feat (3 Bears/WB) — Weight and mass to establish character (Junyer Bear).

Lost and Foundling (Sniffles, Hawk/WB) — Establishing rhythm, slowing it down, as the hawk grows up to the *Overture from William Tell.*

Mr. Mouse Takes a Trip (Mickey, Pluto/Disney) — Establishing a rhythm, altering with secondary actions (Walt Kelly sequence of Mickey running through the train and getting his foot stuck in some baggage).

Out-Foxed (Droopy/MGM) — Clear poses for two characters, good orchestration and timing for readability in Bobe Cannon's wonderful scene of two dogs determining what to do with a shovel.

The Bodyguard (Tom and Jerry/MGM) — Mixed range of emotions between two characters — clear attitude changes, good timing (especially in Irv Spence's "bubble gum" scene).

Jerry's Cousin (Tom and Jerry/MGM) — Two characters designed alike, Jerry and his cousin, defined purely by posture and movement.

The Tender Game (John and Faith Hubley) — Acting with abstract shapes, but still conveying emotion, humor, and personality (masterfully animated by Bobe Cannon, Emery Hawkins, and Jack Schnerk).

Dumbo (Disney) — Emotional content through avoidance of cliché. Bill Tytla's memorable reuniting of mother and son: after their long trunk caress, a lesser animator would go straight to Dumbo breaking down into tears. Tytla's choice to show us Dumbo's elation first, *then* have the tears well up, is brilliance.

Acting in Animation – Part 2: Dialogue

Here we'll concentrate on the broad technical aspects of animating dialogue scenes, having covered most of the theoretical stuff in the previous chapter.

■ Listen to the soundtrack!

Over and over again, in fact, until you have memorized the dialogue perfectly, with all of the accents and nuances intact. Is the dialogue a series of sentences or just one? Do you have to put across a range of emotions, or just a single thought? How do you convey to the audience that your characters are in control of their own thoughts and bodies?

■ Phrasing

Listen to the soundtrack carefully and think of an interesting pattern of movement in which to couch a particular phrase or sentence. This pattern of movement should serve two chief purposes: 1. to make a *visual* equivalent of the highs and lows found in the actor's delivery. 2. To express visually the thought behind the spoken words. It may be helpful to think of phrasing as a musical line (there *is* music to speech patterns) with notes that naturally rise and fall. Many animators find it useful to use a mirror to act out dialogue lines for themselves and then attempt to reproduce their acting in drawings. Others prefer to invent or recall ways of expressing emotions based on experience and intuition. Either way, by phrasing actions around a particular thought, your animation becomes clearer to read and more believable (as opposed to the idea of animating a separate pose for every word and accent). Also, a successful phrasing needn't be contained in a single scene. By straddling a cut between two scenes with one phrase, it gives the impression that the character exists, regardless of where the camera is situated.

■ Acting with the character's entire body

Carrying the idea of phrasing further, bear in mind that it's not just head and hand-flapping, but that the whole body must be used as a means of expression. If the attitude poses you've settled on are strong and readable, then the phrasing patterns you choose should give fluidity and life while reinforcing these poses.

Example: Say you've got two storytelling drawings: one prior to the line "I don't know" (A), and one expressing the thought (B). In the reading, stress is on the word "don't."

"I <u>DON'T</u> KNOW."

By phrasing the action fluidly, you can express the idea and the reading while reinforcing the story poses:

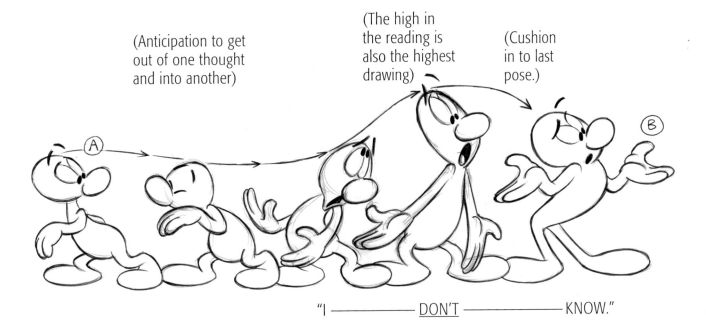

(Anticipation to get out of one thought and into another)

(The high in the reading is also the highest drawing)

(Cushion in to last pose.)

"I ————— DON'T ————— KNOW."

When timing something like this, the less time spent at the beginning of the move, and the more toward the end, the better. This reinforces the pose idea while keeping the character moving.

You may find it useful to think of one pattern of movement while a character is seen to be collecting his thoughts and then hit a strong pose when he actually expresses them.

Example: A character who splutters and stutters before speaking clearly says: "But-but-but how?"

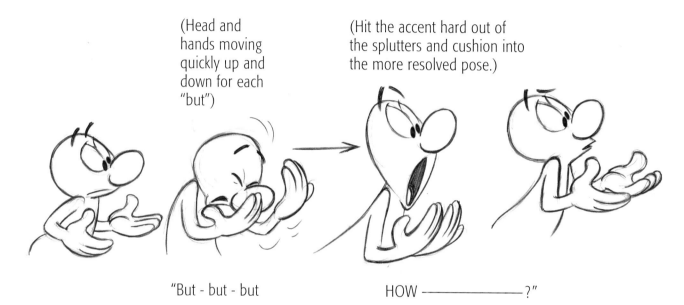

(Head and hands moving quickly up and down for each "but")

(Hit the accent hard out of the splutters and cushion into the more resolved pose.)

"But - but - but   HOW ———————?"

■ Keep your characters sculptural.

Know your character's construction thoroughly and utilize every opportunity to show different angles, head tilts, shifts of weight and posture. It is this quality of three-dimensionality that will ultimately convince your audience that the character is real and tangible. In dialogue scenes, full knowledge of head construction in particular can be used expressively.

Just the tilt of a head can be very expressive if the construction is believable.

"Oh, really?"   "Do tell!"

■ Animating dialogue between two or more characters:

- What contrasting qualities of the different voices can be expressed visually? Perhaps one character is expansive and the other more contained. Or one a clever fast-talker and the other big and stupid. Or one very feminine and one very masculine. One nervous and one confident. Find out the particular qualities of each voice you are dealing with and determine ways of showing these differences to the audience.

- What do you want the audience to see and when? If character "A" speaks, then character "B" responds, "A" shouldn't go into a dead hold until he expresses his next thought. Chances are that "A" would linger on his last thought and then break out of it into repose, *then* react to what "B" is saying. And all of this secondary animation should be subtle enough not to upstage "B," who you want to see saying his line.

Example: Three characters sitting in a circle arguing over directions.

"*I* think we should head west."

"I think we should go back east."

"Well *I* think –

– you're both –

– NUTS!"

The most important factor in this kind of scene is that nothing should occur at the same time. Each reaction should be delayed well behind whoever is making the major move, and the two reacting to the third character should also react on staggered timings to each other. Note how you can get character value out of subtle reactions of the first two getting peeved at each other until both are upstaged and surprised by the third. This kind of subtle weaving in and out of major and minor thoughts is what gives your scene texture and makes it credible for the audience. If every action in the scene were staged and animated with equal intensity, the audience wouldn't know where to look, and the scene would be destroyed.

▪ Using the voice actor's mannerisms:

Often, adopting some of the gestures of the actor providing the character's voice can result in a strong marriage of dialogue and visuals. This partially trades on the audience's awareness of the voice actor's screen persona, and thus sometimes works better with comedy sidekicks than with heroes or heroines. In Disney's Golden Age, no one knew what Verna Felton or Sterling Holloway (or, at Warner's, Mel Blanc) looked like – they were all on *radio*, so the animators had to come up with convincing visuals from the quality of the voice alone, and that's still the way most animation is done. The use of the actor's mannerisms and expressions certainly can work, but it can also be a trap if you go overboard with it.

Personal Examples: *Genie* – I watched Robin Williams' facial expressions, caricatured the Genie's face to be reminiscent of Robin, and wanted to use animation's ability for razor-sharp timing to complement Robin's. I wanted to give the audience the fun of a great Robin performance in cartoon form. However, the Genie's body was completely different (strongman build; hard, bald cranium), not to mention the Hirschfeldian curves. Therefore, I looked at no live-action of Robin's for gestures. (I wanted the Genie to be even wilder – Robin sometimes keeps his arms very close to his body when performing, and he does more with his voice than with his actions – perfect for animators!)

Phil – My earlier designs were like *Taxi*'s Louie de Palma with horns, processed through a Gerald Scarfe blender. John and Ron wanted less of a Danny DeVito caricature, so I pushed him more toward Grumpy from *Snow White and the Seven Dwarfs*. (Okay, so he's the eighth dwarf, "Horny.") When I started animating him, I did a few scenes with very stylized, side-of-the-mouth lip-sync. It worked, but it was too mannered. At the recording session for Phil's song, "One Last Hope," there was a video camera close on Danny's face, and for the first time, I saw Danny's unique consonant shape (particularly for "s") – what I call the "under-the-nose bowtie."

© Disney Enterprises, Inc.

It was such a unique lip shape that I started to incorporate it in the next scene. Hey, presto – all of a sudden, Phil worked.

Rover Dangerfield – Without casting aspersions, this is an example of taking the mannerism thing too far. In practically every scene, they put so much effort into capturing every Rodney nuance, tick, and pop that they lost sight of an overall personality: the "*who*" Rover was, and not the "how he does it." Story problems aside, it's clear they put a lot of good effort into being true to Rodney, but that didn't make Rover a character in his own right.

■ Subtleties in Animation Acting

No one can really teach someone how to be accomplished at the restrained performance. It's largely a matter of personal taste, and the talent to convey your intended acting choices. Here are some thoughts – some performance-based, some technical – that might help.

- Listen to your soundtrack carefully for any accents that can be utilized. If your scene is short, and your movements constrained, you may only have one major accent in it – not several strung together of equal intensity.

- Whenever possible, keep your characters relatively still during character acting scenes. If your scene involves physical activity during dialogue (instead of a talking head shot), try to show the character's emotions through how he performs — it can shed new light on his personality for the audience. If he's reading a book, tying a shoe, or painting a door while he's talking, how he does these things conveys character. Is he concentrating intensely, or is he off-handed about it? Measured? Haphazard? Absent-minded? Is he enjoying the activity or just going through the motions? Are his movements slick? Klutzy? Hesitant?
- Hit your idea poses strongly, but then work out subtle complexities within the pose.

"Oh, no!"   "Please! Please go away!"

In this example, the character is shocked by someone he's trying to avoid. He flies into **B** ("Oh, no!") by the time we hear the word "oh." Once he's in this pose, he shivers in fear within the pose. Also, "no" is louder on the track, so his head accent reflects this within the major pose. He slumps into **C** on the first "please." Once there, his hand massages his forehead, while his other hand makes feeble waving gestures to shoo away the offending party. Make sure to give your audience enough screen time to read your acting. Don't pass through the poses and secondary actions so quickly that none of them land.

- Make your spacing contained enough for changes of expression to read. Example: You've decided to make the character's eyebrows wriggle, and you've worked it out perfectly. However, you've animated it on a head movement that is spaced more broadly than your wriggle – you'll never see the wriggle, because it's moving in smaller increments than the overall movement on the whole head. Instead, use a moving hold or series of tracebacks for the head, during which you move the brows – which leads us to our next point…

- Restrict movement generally to the area you want the audience to see. If you want the audience to watch an eye movement, don't have the arms flapping around at the same time.

- Avoid even timing, especially on expression changes. If you go mechanically through the X–sheets and make a new drawing every eight frames, you'll wind up with mush when it's inbetweened. Figure out timings for your actions and poses either in seconds (or parts thereof) or for the duration of a spoken phrase. Don't be afraid to get to your "idea" pose with a minimum of drawings, and then work within and around the pose. Even thinking on twos as a general habit can be limiting if you want your timing to have fluidity and snap. The great Disney animation is always a combination of ones and twos in an acting scene, almost never totally ones or totally twos. This adds texture and weight to the timing, and when it's done well and spaced correctly, your viewer (yes, even the animation geeks) shouldn't be able to tell when it switches back and forth.

- Think of unusual ways to get an idea across that will be entertaining to watch – unusual mouth shapes and positions, interesting eye and brow combinations and altering of eye shapes, use of eyelids and underlids, finger and hand gestures, and of course body posture used expressively.

- Consider the cumulative effect of all of the different traits that will define the character's personality. In other words, instead of trying to pack a zillion different attitudes into a three-foot scene, settle on one or two key emotions per scene, and let the total effect of all the combined scenes shape an impression in the audience's mind.

- Observe and absorb! Watch as much as you can in live-action, animation, and life itself to understand the different and unique ways that people and animals express themselves. Log this information mentally or in sketches to utilize later. Although I'm a firm believer in avoiding the cliché, a comprehensive knowledge of cartoon and graphically drawn expressions can be invaluable. (And at least, if you know the clichés, then you know your starting point if you want to go in a different direction.) Here's a fun experiment: Video-record something relatively dull and static, like a talk show, and play it back at high speed. You'll see the participants click sharply into different poses and attitudes.

Optional Exercise: Take this pair of eyes (eyes only!) and draw key positions for this line of dialogue:

"OH! I – uh – er – I didn't – Nice day, isn't it?"

Recommended Cartoons

Hold the Lion, Please (Bugs, Lion/WB) — Ken Harris' animation of the lion's hen-pecked telephone call is a great example of keeping the head sculptural.

My Favorite Duck (Porky, Daffy/WB) — Phrasing, acting with the entire body, as shown in Bobe Cannon's Daffy speech at the end, as he acts out the rest of the cartoon against a white field.

Mickey's Rival (Mickey, Minnie, Mortimer/Disney) — Minnie goes gaga over Mortimer, her dialogue phrasing straddles cuts from long shot to close-up by cutting in to a smaller field.

Falling Hare (Bugs, Gremlin/WB) — Bob McKimson's masterful animation of Bugs reading "Victory Through Hare Power" is a sterling example of keeping the character sculptural and three-dimensionally convincing.

Song of the South (Brers Fox, Bear, and Rabbit/Disney) — This one has it all: contrasting character types, multi-dialogue scenes with shifting points of interest, fantastic phrasing, character acting based on each individual personality and how they relate to one another.

Alice in Wonderland (Disney) — Ward Kimball's Mad Tea Party shows masterful adapting of character mannerisms based on voice artists Ed Wynn and Jerry Colonna.

The Jungle Book (Disney) — Milt Kahl's "interrogation" scene between Shere Khan and Kaa: complete understanding of the contrasting personalities through their individual movements, directing the audiences' eye through back-and-forth dialogue, mastery of head and body construction used for attitude and expression. (See "Lip-Sync" chapter for more about this.)

Character Construction and Design

Most "traditional" cartoon-character construction is based on circles and pear-shapes, as these tend to be easier to turn around and more fluid to animate. It doesn't necessarily mean that all shapes slosh around without any anatomy underneath, however, unless you're working for Fleischer's in the 1930's. "Cute" characters tend to have larger heads in relation to the rest of their bodies.

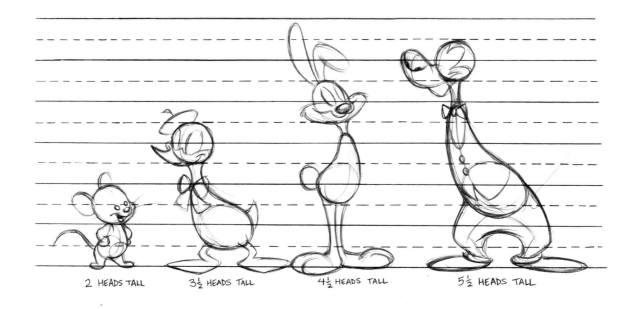

2 HEADS TALL   3½ HEADS TALL   4½ HEADS TALL   5½ HEADS TALL

Posture is a good place to start for good acting and poses. It's good to start with a simple line of action that establishes attitude, on which you can build the character (not unlike a wire armature for a clay sculpture).

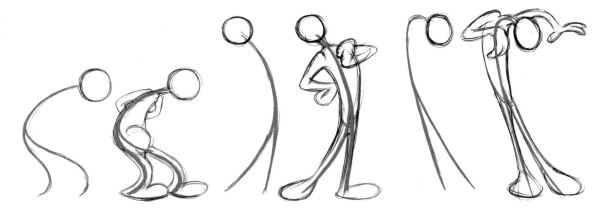

Although these simple shapes can be animated fluidly, be aware of at least a simple skeletal structure underneath on which the fleshy bits hang. Some animators (Art Babbitt, for example) would even have it that your character should work in this skeletal form without embellishment, if your animation is "correct," the theory being that the animation should work primarily due to "successive breaking of joints" for its fluidity, and not through Olive Oyl rubberizing.

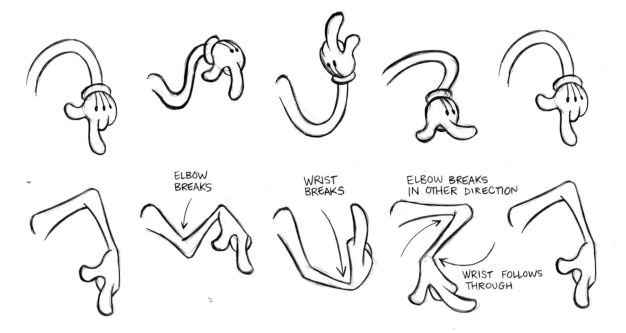

Even though you're animating cartoons, the knowledge of human anatomy is very helpful, as the same muscles and bones that would be well-defined in a good life drawing would be defined (and perhaps *re*fined) in a cartoon drawing. For example, bony parts that don't have much muscle around them, and are closer to the surface of the skin, benefit from definition in your animation: shoulders, elbows, wrists, knuckles, knees, heels, ankles, and a feeling for a ribcage and a pelvis underneath all help make your character "feel" convincing to an audience.

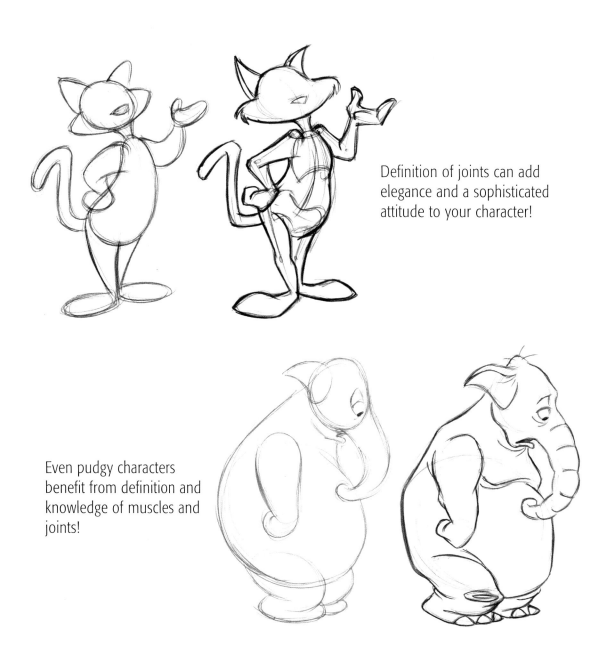

Definition of joints can add elegance and a sophisticated attitude to your character!

Even pudgy characters benefit from definition and knowledge of muscles and joints!

Hand construction

Most cartoon hands tend to be rubbery and doughy, based on a circle for the palm and rubber fingers connected to it.

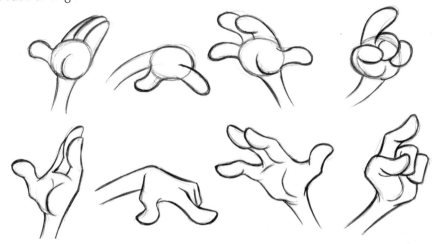

Further definition, however, can be an added bonus. The above hands obviously aren't anatomically correct, but the more defined joints do add a feeling of structure and reality.

Bear in mind that, although hands carry a great deal of detailed information, it's best to simplify them in medium to long shots so they don't look unnaturally defined in relation to the rest of the design. Feet tend to be a bit neglected, but it's a good idea to have them constructed with at least the same feeling of underneath structure as the hands, so they look consistent within the design.

Here, the hands are too complex, and the feet are not designed to match.

These hands work better with the overall design.

Now the feet match the anatomy indicated in the hands.

Facial construction

Although the muscles and skin coverings all over the head are flexible, some parts look better in distortion than others. If you can retain a feeling of a solid cranium underneath, with more flexible jowls and eye muscles, your animation will be more believable than that which regularly distorts the cranium.

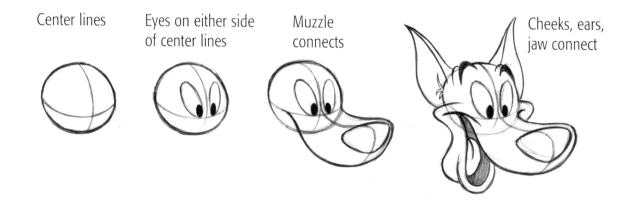

Center lines   Eyes on either side of center lines   Muzzle connects   Cheeks, ears, jaw connect

With a system like this based on simple shapes, it's easy to visualize the head in different angles and expressions.

Some cranial distortion is allowable, but it should not be left on screen long enough to be perceived as a goony drawing.

Recoil quickly into more "normal" construction!

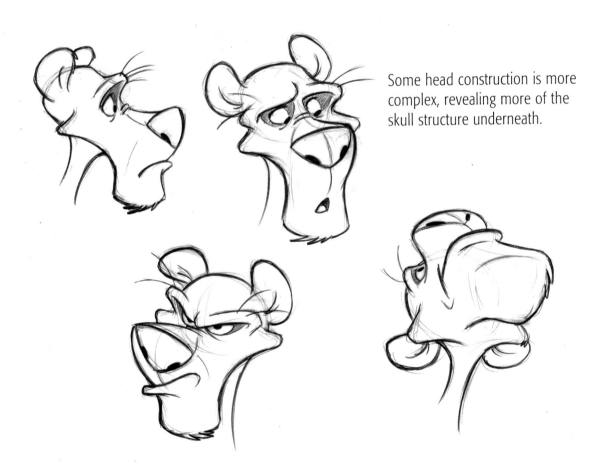

Some head construction is more complex, revealing more of the skull structure underneath.

Cute characters tend to have large craniums and small mouths.

Tough characters tend toward small craniums and large jaws.

More info of this type is found in the classic Preston Blair animation book.

A word about "angular" character design:

Don't let it throw you! In most cases, you can still use circular cartoon construction for your rough stages. If your animation has the right squash and stretch, breaking of joints, overlap, timing, etc., you can impose the niceties of angular design later when you tie down your roughs. (Of course, if you can do it all at once, bearing angular construction in mind as you animate, even better!)

Character Design

- Has the overall style of the film been determined? If it has, try to design your characters to reflect and complement that style (i.e., traditional or graphic, sparse backgrounds or fully rendered, etc.?) If lighting plays an important part in the film, will your characters be dimensional enough to show those effects? If they're design-y, is there a design-y approach to how they're lit that will satisfy the requirements? Is there a medium, large, or minuscule budget on the film? Can you design the characters to reflect that budget (i.e., number of colors, amount of pencil-pushing required, number of characters in most scenes)?

- How reality-based do your characters need to be? Are your characters in physical situations? Natural settings? Do they need to convince an audience that they exist perfectly in three dimensions? How can you use anatomy to define your characters? Can your characters be looser or more graphic with an understanding of a logical anatomy?

- Details — Concentrate areas of detail where you want the audience to look. What facial and clothing details are necessary to define your characters? Instead of settling on lots of fussy, decorative trappings, try to conceive the characters simply and make the animation work harder to define the physical properties and attitudes.

- Design your characters with the intent to pose them strongly — the fussier the detail, the less inclined you'll be to animate them dynamically, and the less an audience will read your attitudes. If the characters are a bit more streamlined, the tendency is to make their poses a bit more streamlined as well.

■ If the film has several characters, design them to all live in the same world together. An overall approach to angularity, curviness, eye definition, hands, mouth shapes, and consistency of anatomy will help give the film a unified look.

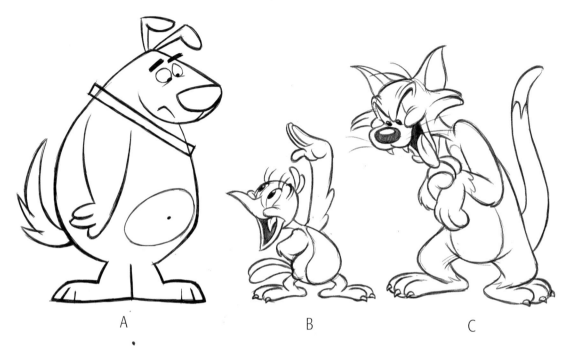

A   B   C

Character A doesn't live in the same world as B… but C does.

■ Color – Have colors been chosen to suit the environment the characters will perform in? Are there too many colors to read them against the BG? Do the character colors read in a number of situations in the film? Do they need to alter for a particular scene?

■ Appeal! Very elusive to define but probably the most important subject! Here are a few ideas to chew on:

- Round shapes and pear-shapes are comfortable to look at. Angular shapes are more difficult to look at but are perceived as more sophisticated.
- Eyes slightly crossed (but not so much that they need corrective lenses) give the character focus. Features radiating outward from the nose are usually more appealing than disjointed ones. Also, any amount of pliability in features (how soft they appear) in facial muscles, hands, clothing, etc., adds to appeal.

Fig. 1   Fig. 2

In Fig. 1, a prototypical 30's character, all the features are lined up on perpendicular axes, making the result stiff-looking.

In Fig. 2, more of a 40's kinda guy, features radiate outward from the nose connection point. Eyes are slightly crossed (for focus) and pupils protrude slightly. Cheeks also protrude off of the main circle, and the whole thing is more organically drawn to exaggerate the pliability and fleshiness.

- Angles and defined shapes of even the smallest details can make a huge difference!

Fig. 3   Fig. 4

In Fig. 3, the pupil is just a bland dot, looking in no particular direction. The eyebrow is a straight slash bisected by the forehead, the mouth is a smooth but uninteresting curve.

In Fig. 4, the pupil is elongated, and now *angled* to show where he's looking. The eyebrow, drawn with more flair, has more weight and length beyond the forehead. The addition of a smile line and a crinkle to the mouth gives more quirky character.

- Body details should be compatible with facial details — clothing too! (In other words, if you are doing "40's pliable," for example, fingers, feet, body shapes should reflect that pliability as well as the face.)

Above, a little exercise: I've designed a cartoon mouse for a classic 40's chase cartoon, a retro graphic TV spot, a 1970's wiggly line short, and an "adult" TV sitcom. Try this with your own characters from different periods and film styles.

Drawing in Animation

Finding the poses – What communicates best? What communicates best and is also unexpected? Try to arrive at *storytelling* drawings – not necessarily the ones that will be your broadest extremes, but rather those that will telegraph to an audience the "story" of your scene (the previously-mentioned "Name that Tune" technique).

Then elaborate the action with further keys and breakdowns. (Of course, some scenes will work better posed-out, and others are better straight-ahead.)

Go for the *feeling* first, anatomy second!! This works for both cartoony and straight characters (although *knowledge* of their anatomy is essential!). Make your drawings support the *idea* of the pose – so all elements work organically to portray movement and flexibility. Understand how overlap in your animation will strengthen its communicative power!

© Disney Enterprises, Inc.

This pose concentrates on anatomy first: everything is well-constructed, limbs connect in all the right places, head structure is solid.

This pose goes for feeling first: everything supports the "point."

Now, the anatomy comes in when the pose is tied down. Everything connects where it should, but the entire figure is drawn to support the idea of the pose, including the overall arc of body and overlapping elements.

Everything you draw or conceive should have a sense of "give" to it — that all of a character's body parts affect each other, and that they all have an inherent elasticity. Everything is in a constant state of motion, and even tiny movements indicating recoil, follow-through, and settling of overlap all contribute to the effect of your character being alive.

Loosening up!

Here are some points to consider if you're feeling your work is a bit stiff-looking.

■ Work roughly, with attention to basic construction but not final detail when keying out a scene. Animate in a straight-ahead fashion from beginning to end of the scene, even though you're posing — this way you'll find various peaks and resolutions that come "organically" as you're drawing. In other words, instead of drawing keys disconnected in thought that you then attempt to connect:

Animate in a more straight-ahead way that follows the flow of movement.

All of the above can be called "keys"; even though there are twice the drawings, each is of equal importance in defining the flow and thrust of the movement.

■ Drag and Overlap

Practically any movement will benefit from a little anticipation, drag, and overlap – including "realistic" movement – as long as the degree to which they are used complements the style and brief. Generally, the quicker or broader the action, the more extreme the drag. If the *direction of thrust* is borne in mind when animating, the drag should come naturally.

Drag on a human head turn:

Dead-in-the-middle inbetween

Tilt the head down, change the angle
of the axis, lead with the cranium.

Drag and overlap on hair:

Drag on clothing:

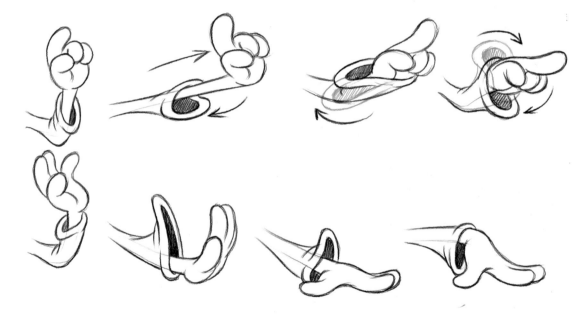

Drag and overlap on floppy appendages:

Drag on major body movements:

Try to wrest every opportunity for drag out of even "simple" movements:

Instead of making direct paths of movement for mushy action —

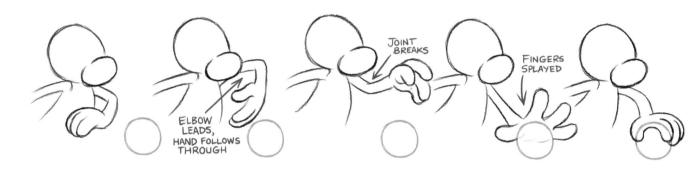

— make a movement that has to go up first before it comes down — i.e., one that takes full advantage of animation's fluidity.

Try some drag on the entire body, not just parts of it, as in the above sequence, where the head leads, and the body follows through.

Drag on facial muscles:

If you treat the cranium as relatively solid, and the mouth and jowls as loose and plastic, your face animation should become more fluid without looking unbelievable.

■ Clean-up and Tie-down

The clean-up process in traditional animation can often result in making animation appear stiffer — but that has less to do with the talent of the clean-up artists (and I humbly sing their praises here) than with much rough animation not having the nuances worked out in the tied-down roughs before it's handed off. When I worked in commercials, much of my animation was inked, so I trained myself to "clean-up for inking" — loose enough to keep it alive, tied-down enough for an inker to follow accurately, like the 40's and 50's shorts guys used to do. It's still my preferred way of working, regardless of whether I hand it over to a clean-up artist for the final line (and who are far better at it than I will ever be). For the purposes of discussion, then, I'll refer to such drawings as "tie-downs," since that should really be part of the animation process itself.

Don't kill your loose animation when putting a clean line around it! If anything, exaggerate the feeling of looseness by taking the tie-downs even farther than your roughs. Here's a nice loose series of roughs:

These tie-downs flatten the animation — the single line is a tracing, not a line that defines form. The line weight is perfectly even, and the hair is too repetitive in its separate shapes.

These are better: The varied weight of the line gives mass to nose and jowls; tapered eyelashes give personality. A feeling of flesh growing out of flesh is better-defined (lip into jowl, jowl into cranium, etc.). Hair is not tied down into regular, even patterns. Shapes are defined for their uniqueness — one round pupil, one elongated pupil, etc.

To avoid stiff tie-downs, the following is helpful:

- You will almost always get a better drawing if your roughs are sketched lightly and your tie-downs are on top of them in the same pencil. If you rough first in blue, or tie-down on a separate sheet, you're breaking the drawing process into two chunks, thought of individually. By working directly over your roughs in the same pencil, you're going through the process of making *one* good drawing, which has form and three dimensions built up — like sculpting! If you like to work very loosely, and your drawings are too grubby to work on top of, that's okay — trace light transfers of them onto new sheets, then build up a good tie-down over your light construction lines.

- Don't forget the drag, overlap, and squash and stretch you've put into your roughs. Emphasize them even more, bearing in mind direction of thrust – again, easier to do over light roughs!

- Consider the value of the weight of your line. Knowledge of "thick and thin" when drawing adds solidity, particularly on rounded shapes. A thicker line on the underside of jowls, noses, lower lips, etc., gives those rounded shapes more three-dimensional believability. Thicker eyelids and lashes can give character and personality.

- When drawing shapes of similar texture (hair, for example), don't regularize. The hair in the first series of tie-downs is too similar in repeated shapes to be interesting. The hair in the second series has a more varied – and, thus, interesting – pattern. However, these variations must follow through properly in the animation whenever possible, instead of just boiling around randomly.

Another valuable tip for further loosening up is in timing: if your broader actions are on ones (even just a short burst of them) and your cushions, moving holds, or tracebacks are left on twos, it gives the work texture in timing – and also means that not everything needs to be put on ones to appear loose! Sometimes this technique can even be used in CG, particularly in scenes where 2-D animation is blended with 3-D, to make all the elements live in the same world (example: the Tiger's Head cave in Disney's *Aladdin*).

TechNiquE

The Exposure Sheet

The traditional hand-numbered paper Exposure Sheet ("X-sheet" for short) is fast becoming a relative of the dodo. With the advent of more CG animation, Flash, and paperless systems, the traditional X-sheet is frequently an afterthought, if it is indeed used at all. This is a crime to the art, in my opinion, because the X-sheet is not only the document that can act as the "bible" for almost all stages of an animated scene (from editor, to director, to layout artist, to animator, to clean-up artist, to scanner, to painter, to cameraman or scene planner, to final compositor), but it is also the perfect visual guide for an animator to plan his or her scene creatively and efficiently. In the current scenario, the best I can do is map out for you how a traditional X-sheet works, and hope for the future that it continues to be incorporated into the animation process.

Here is a standard
X-sheet:

PROD.	SEQ.	SCENE							SHEET

ACTION	DIAL	5	4	3	2	1	BG	CAMERA INSTRUCTIONS
1								
2								
3								
4								
5								
6								

It is normally 6 feet long (96 frames) — not an actual foot, but the representation of an actual 12 inches of 35mm film that would measure out to 16 frames. It is subdivided horizontally, with each horizontal row representing one frame of picture, with darker horizontal lines every 8 frames for easy reference. "1st sheets" often have only 5 feet of information (80 frames), utilizing the top space for more detailed scene identification and camera instruction. The X-sheet is subdivided vertically into several thin columns, and they are read right to left, with the right side devoted to camera instructions, the middle for the BG, underlay, overlay, and animation levels, and the far left for the dialogue breakdown, music indications, and directorial and timing information.

Camera Instructions

On the right side of the sheet, all of the information needed for fielding, camera movement, and exposures (fades, dissolves) is exposed. Let's say that you would like Scene 1 to start at 15 field center, hold that position for the first foot, then truck in to 10 Field, 1 North, 2 East over 28 frames, and hold that position for 30 frames to the end of the scene. You want the truck-in to cushion out smoothly from your start position and cushion in smoothly to the final position. Also, you would like a 12-frame fade-in at the head of the scene, and a 12-frame dissolve to Scene 2 at the end of the scene. The right column of your X-sheet would look like this:→

The cut points (start and end of the scene) are marked in red horizontally. The opening field is shown on the sheets and held, with a straight vertical line, to the point where the truck-in starts. The wiggly line indicates the cushion out, then a constant trucking rate, finished off with the opposite wiggly line to indicate the cushion to a stop for the final fielding, over the desired 28-frame range. The final field is marked and held to the end of the scene. The 12-frame fade-in is indicated by the upside-down widening "V." (A fade-out is a right-side up closing "V".) The 24-frame dissolve at the end is shown as a fade-out V superimposed over a fade-in V to show the overlap between Scenes 1 and 2. You should understand when animating that the following scene also requires the same degree of overlap at the head, and that you must provide animation for the entire length of the dissolve in both scenes. However, the usual readability of images through a dissolve is up to the center of the dissolve for the outgoing scene, and *from* the center of the dissolve for the incoming scene.

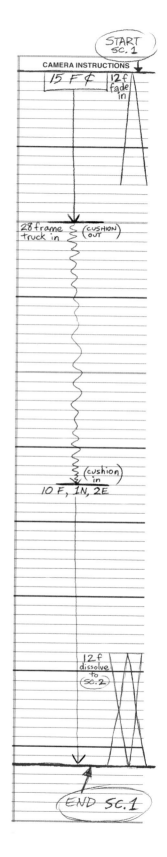

The Dialogue and Action Columns

On the far left side of the X-sheet are the Dialogue and Action indications. In the dialogue column, the soundtrack has been broken down by the editor for every frame, showing exactly how many frames it takes to make the sounds for the individual words. In this example, where the character Finky is saying, "Hey, Renfrew…. Over here!" we can see that it takes 1 frame for the "R" in Renfrew, 3 frames for the "eh," 1 frame for the "n," 2 frames for the "f," 2 frames for the "r," and 12 frames that trail out for the "ew." (More about lip-sync and dialogue animation later!) This column is often used for music and hard sound effects as well, indicating the frequency of beats and appearance of accents. We can see here that the beats are coming 12 frames apart, with a "ricochet" noise occurring on one of the beats. In the action column, the director has placed his timing notes for the major movement and acting of the character: he hops in on 12's to match the beats (but to make it look funnier, the "ups" are what hits the beats), and he's "happy" while he's doing it. He then anticipates (rears back) with squinted eyes, and zips out of frame to match the "ricochet" noise. Moreover, if the director hasn't already made these indications, it's up to the animator to plan the X-sheets in similar fashion, to establish and break rhythms, and do a lot of the thinking work about the scene before the animation even begins. I can't place enough importance on this stage of animation planning, because it allows the animator to see, visually on paper, how the rhythms and changes in timing and acting can work. It's literally the "road map" for the execution of the scene.

The Animation Levels

Between the left and right sides are the animation columns, read from right to left, with the bottom-most level on the right, and the topmost level on the left. Although this was originally conceived as a guide for the cameraman (indicating from bottom to top what order the various cels, BGs and overlay/underlay artwork had to be stacked for the frame to appear correctly on screen), it is still used to this day on digital exposure sheets for proper alignment of all levels.

From right to left, we see that BG 7 is on the bottom, followed by the neon sign that fades on for 8 frames, holds for 8 frames, and fades out for 8 frames, followed by a blank (indicated by the "X"), before the 32-frame cycle starts up again. On top of that are cast shadows, then the character Finky on top. This is followed by an effects level (dust) that pops on for the "zip." Finally, at the topmost level is an overlay (a foreground piece of art) labeled "OL-7."

Each level is prefixed by a logical letter set before the numbers: "N" for neon, "S" for shadows, "F" for Finky, etc. The sheets are numbered on twos with odd numbers (1, 3, 5, etc.), except at the end, where ones are used for more elaborate movement on the anticipation and zip-out. An excellent working method is to number the sheets on twos all the way down, usually in the major character level. (This is regardless of whether you will eventually need ones or not.) This way, you can see exactly which frame number corresponds to dialogue, beats, and timing indications.

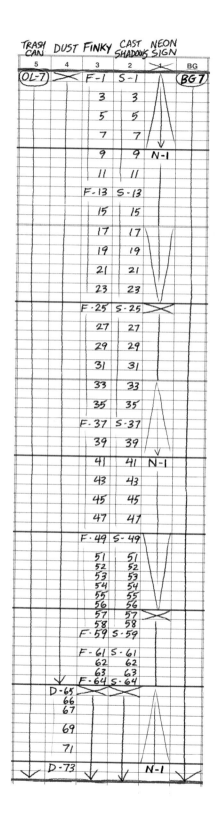

Now here's the
whole kaboodle:

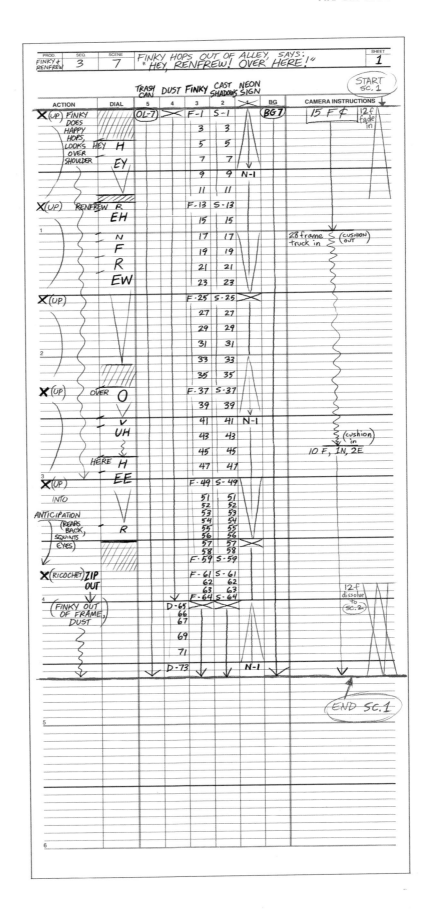

There are even more variations and notations to be made on the X-sheet, especially once it is converted to a digital format. Here, panning and trucking increments can be notated, as can exposures for certain levels (say, a translucency on the cast shadows and tone mattes), and further stuff too technical for me to understand or mention here. In any event, you will continue to see references to the humble traditional X-sheet throughout the rest of the chapters.

Layout and Staging

Animators need to have a good working knowledge of the mechanics of film and film composition to understand how these tools of communication can best support their performances (and how the performances can be engineered to complement the filmic concepts).

Film Grammar: Types of Shots

Establishing Shot – shows the overall setting (and perhaps characters involved) to define for the audience the place, the time of day, and the atmosphere of the sequence.

Medium Shot (M.S.) – shot that shows characters' full bodies in a framing spacious enough to include reasonable background (and possibly foreground) detail.

Long Shot (L.S.) – camera is far away from subject matter, characters quite small in frame.

Close-Up (C.U.) – close detail shot (often facial) with little or no extraneous background detail.

[Also "Medium Close-Up" (M.C.U.) – say, a waist-up shot of characters, and "Medium Long Shot" (M.L.S.) – characters farther away than in a medium shot, but not tiny, plus Extreme C.U. and Extreme L.S.]

P.O.V. (point of view) Shot – composed and staged as if the audience is experiencing the shot first-hand through the character's eyes.

Crane Shot – shot with shifting composition (height of camera, distance from subject matter, turning around a character or stationary object), so called because of the hydraulic crane required to execute such a shot in live-action.

Panning Shot, or Pan – which has the camera moving up, down, or across the scene, either to follow the action of a character, or to establish a scene and "locate" the focus of attention.

Trucking Shots – "Truck In" shots are used to zero in on an area of developing importance as the scene unfolds. "Truck Out" shots are used to reveal things of developing importance in the surrounding area originally outside the field of vision. In live-action, executed with telephoto lenses instead of physically moving the camera (also known as "Zoom In" and "Zoom Out").

Cutaway – cut to a reaction shot of a second character (other than the one performing or speaking).

Tracking Shot – follows a character's action throughout a scene.

Dolly Shot – like a truck-in or -out, but executed with the camera on tracks to get closer to or farther away from the subject (as opposed to doing it solely with the lenses), giving more depth and changing background perspective.

Scene transitions:

Cut – most often-used way of changing scenes: one scene finishes, and the next follows, butted up against it.

Fade – establishes a passage of time. "Fade out / fade in" means one thought or sequence ends / a new one begins at a later time. "Fade in" opens a sequence and determines the start of a new idea. "Fade out" is the "period" at the end, which says that the sequence or chain of ideas has been completed.

Dissolve – also establishes a passage of time, but because the two scenes overlap, it usually denotes a *shorter* lapse of time than fade out / fade in (unless the dissolve is quite long). Dissolves can also be used to compress time (when two scenes are too short to convey an idea, the dissolve lengthens *both* of them).

Wipe – an animated, optically printed, or digitally created device that obliterates the existing scene and reveals the next (sometimes seen as a "clock"), which also denotes passage of time.

"Whip" pan – high-speed blurred pan that moves rapidly away from the existing scene to the new scene – often in a completely different area or time, the blur "fudging" the geography between the two.

"Jump Cut" – a mistake that occurs when one scene directly follows another and repeats elements from it only marginally differently, thus resulting in a "jump." (Cuts work best when their composition, size of subject, and camera angle are markedly different from each other.)

Layout

The layout artists in animation are truly the cinematographers. They determine the best ways to convey a story point, mood, or action piece, through the use of camera movement and placement, lighting, composition, and cutting from scene to scene. Animators don't necessarily need to know the finer points, but working knowledge is essential, since it has a direct impact on how the animation is executed. Also, there will probably be many times when you need to create your own layouts for a variety of reasons, so what follows is a run-down of things to consider, both when animating and when conceiving your own layouts.

■ Mechanics

Below are field charts used in standard traditional animation:

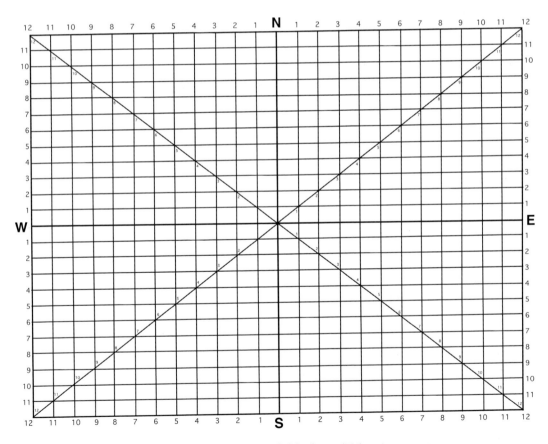

Standard 12-Field Chart (TV)

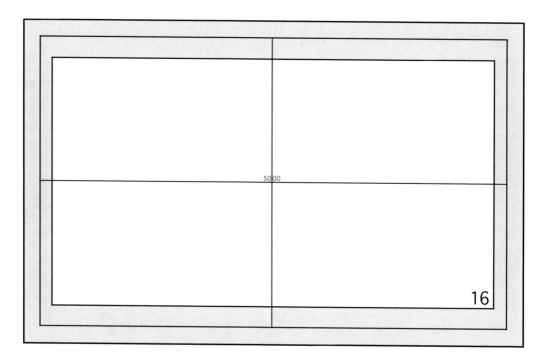

35mm Widescreen Chart for 16-Field (Cinema)

These grids are the road map for the framing and camera movement within a scene. Since many studios have proprietary grids and numbering systems for feature work, we'll concentrate on the standard 12-Field for now. Regardless of the numbers, however, the principles of indicating fielding are the same.

Example 1:

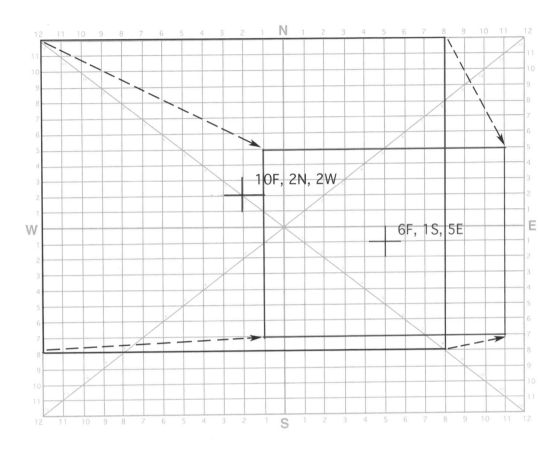

Here's a move that starts at 10 Field, 2 fields North, and 2 fields West of center (10F, 2N, 2W) and trucks in to 6 Field, 1 field South, and 5 fields East (6F, 1S, 5E). From the exposure sheet, you can see that this move takes 6 feet (96 frames, or 4 seconds). When the grid is placed over the BG Layout and character poses, it's clear that the camera is following the character as he walks, while also getting closer to him.

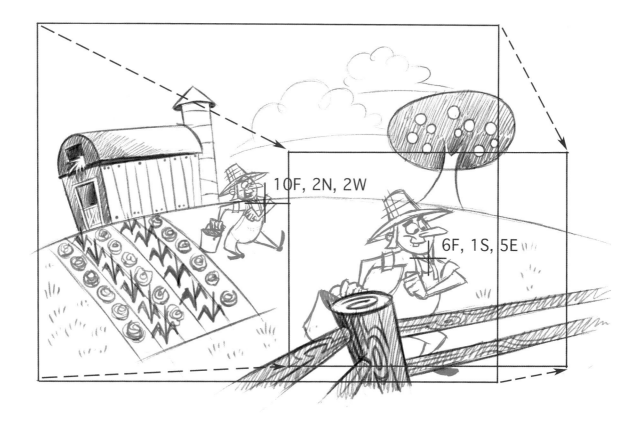

As an animator, you would understand that your character needs to be animated on ones for this scene, because leaving him on twos while the camera pans across on ones will result in "strobing," an onscreen vibration caused by the fact that, on twos, the character would lag behind for every other frame. You would also need to establish a rhythm for the character's steps (say, 8 steps at 12 frames per step) that would ensure that he arrives at the right spot by the end of the scene.

Example 2:

Here's a layout that goes from 12F¢ to 10F, 1N, 1W, over 4 feet, 8 frames (72 frames, or 3 seconds). From this, you can make the judgment call that your animation can stay primarily on twos. Because this is a slow truck-in, which will appear as a "drift," the camera move increments will be very close together, meaning that there will be no perceptible strobing in the character.

Example 3:

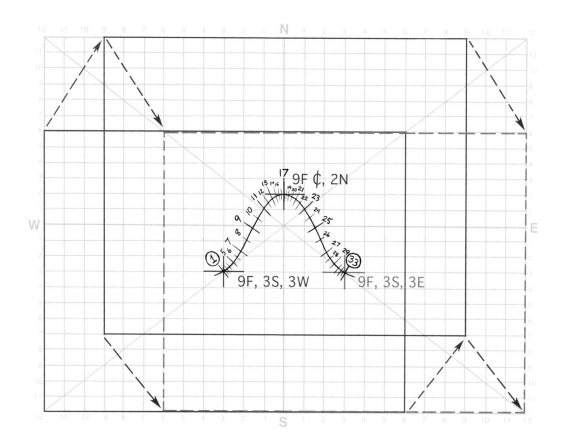

Above is a move that starts at 9F, 3S, 3W, pans up to 9F¢, 2N, and pans down to 9F, 3S, 3E, all along a plotted curve over a 2-foot duration (32 frames, with the move stopping on frame 33). The reason for the curve is that it will result in a much more natural, fluid move than if there were merely two straight lines between the points. When animating the scene, it's obvious that the peak of the jump should occur at the highest point of the camera move. After the scene is roughed-in, you can even plot the points yourself to ensure that the move works precisely with your animation:

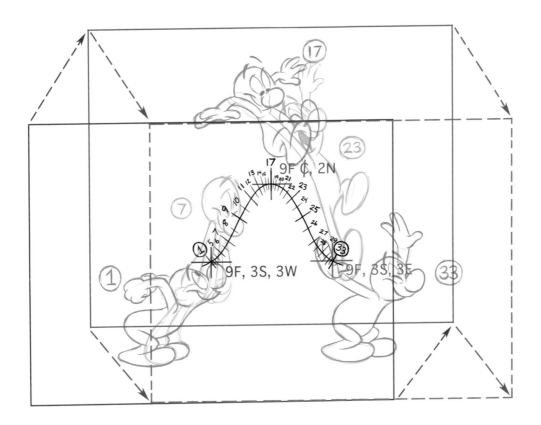

You can see that I've planned a cushion-out (where the spacing of the move accelerates), a slow-in / slow-out at the peak of the curve (to accommodate the more close-together drawings at the highest part of the jump), another acceleration out of the peak, and finally a cushion-in (deceleration) to the final position. These plotted points are the centers of each new fielding for every frame of the move. In other words, to find out how your character appears on a specific frame number, line up a plotted point with the corresponding animation drawing and put the 9 Field around it, with the point as 9 Field Center. Further embellishments you might plan would be for the animation at the beginning to slightly precede the move (imitating a live-action cameraman attempting to catch up with the action), and then at the other end have the move slightly precede the animation to more clearly read the character's landing.

You will encounter many more situations like these as you animate; the more well-versed you are in these mechanics, the more you can ensure that your animation communicates your intentions for the scene.

■ Composition

- Consider the design of the overall frame — what makes a pleasing combination of large and small shapes, light and dark, angles and straights against curves, etc.? Not everything that is important must be center-screen; often a major character can look better in a composition to one side or another, if the BG elements are designed to lead your eye to him.

- Allow certain areas of the layout to be less cluttered so your characters are in a visually "quiet" area of the frame for maximum readability. Don't compose a BG layout without considering character placement and movement; you can make a very pleasing and artful BG layout that works well by itself but looks lousy on film when characters are placed on it. Also, the length of screen time has direct bearing on the amount of detail you can include — the longer the scene, the more chance the audience has to see interesting details; the shorter the scene, the simpler the composition should be.

- Consider the characters themselves as compositional design elements: their shapes, sizes, and placement may be the major design points of a scene (especially a group scene).

Instead of a dull composition like this…

… try a dynamically staged one like this!

Further examples:

And of course, in TV commercials, TV cutoff must be considered, and cinema cutoff for the movies, to ensure that a TV broadcast or slightly-off cinema screen won't delete important scene information.

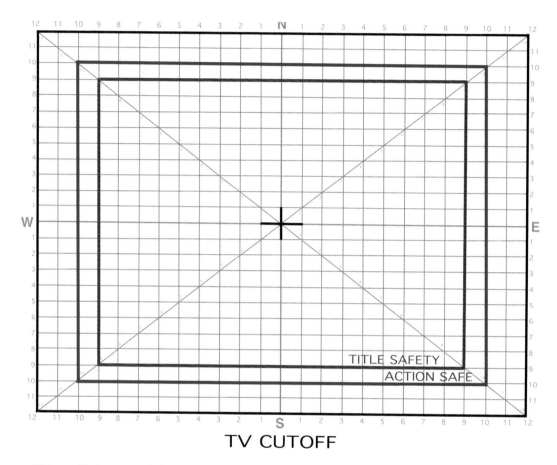

TV CUTOFF

TV cutoff: On a 12-Field grid, "Title Safety" is about 3 fields in (9 Field Center), "Action Safe" is about 2 fields in (10 Field Center).

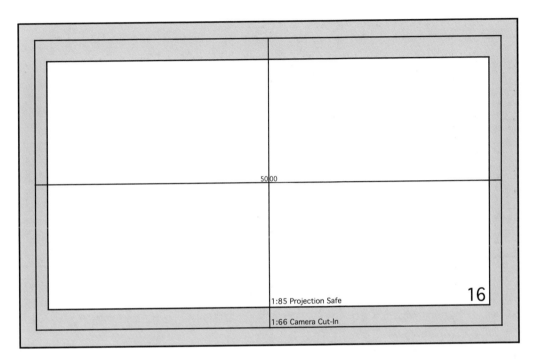

35mm "widescreen" cutoff: Note that there is the full field indicated, as well as "Projection Safe" to allow for the difference between projectors in a variety of venues.

■ Geography

Establish an overall plan of the environment in which your characters will be moving (perhaps a top view and a front view) and imagine the camera stationed around it to give the various shots needed in the sequence. Most filmmakers prefer not to break the 180° arc:

Where you place the camera depends on how elaborate your staging should be for readability and visual interest:

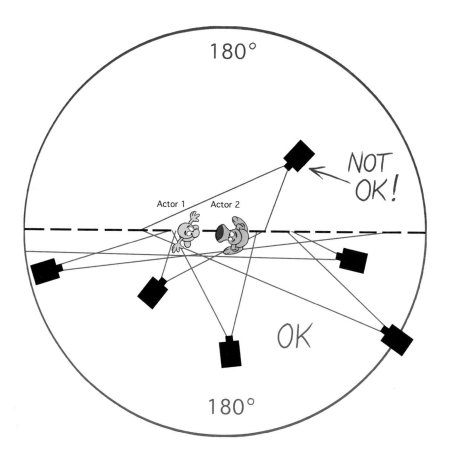

- "Proscenium arch" — Imagine the set like a theater stage, where all the action takes place behind the proscenium arch and imagine the camera panning, cutting from close-up to long shot, etc., directly in front of the action. This is the simplest form of camera placement.

- More elaborate framing requires more consideration of various elements. Establish screen direction: If your characters are moving and facing from left to right, don't throw in a scene where the character relationships are thrown into complete reverse; it will look as if the characters are swapping places in the room rather than the camera changing its point of view. Even if your camera placement differs radically from scene to scene, screen direction can be the cohesive element.

Example:

Top view of character running in desert

M.C.U. of character center screen while BG pans past

Character runs down into distance, having entered from screen left.

By keeping the screen direction generally left to right, these scenes cut together fluidly even though the camera placement shifts radically. But imagine audience confusion if the second scene were flopped:

Establish logic of camera placement: If, for example, you're dealing with small char-acters, you may want the camera close to the ground with them at all times. If your sequence deals with speed (a typical Road Runner chase, for example), you may want a succession of scenes with characters center-screen and BGs rushing past (rather than interrupting the flow with, say, one scene in the middle of the action with a stationary camera and the characters whizzing past the lens). If you want a "fragmented," offbeat look, you may want to use discontinuous scenes with a variety of angles. Or, as with the runner, you may want to make a series of interestingly composed shots with the move-ment of the character as the logical thread that holds the sequence together.

Do you want a moving or a stationary shot? Basically, the camera needn't move unless it is integral to telling the story. Don't stick in a 5-field truck-in when getting closer to the character doesn't illuminate the scene any further. Don't cut back and forth, in and out, just for the sake of moving the camera around. The exception is a gentle "moving camera," quiet 1- or 2-field trucks or pans that take the edge off the hard cuts and lend production value.

Staging

Staging in animation is about communicating effectively to your audience, utilizing elements of layout, background, composition, and organization of characters.

A large part of staging is layout and film grammar: knowing when to use a close-up, when to pan, when to truck in or out, when to cut from one scene to another. Much of this can be learned from watching live-action editing and seeing how the camera is placed (and why!). Knowing how screen geography works is also a necessary tool.

■ Staging Your Characters

- Who has the main action in the scene? If it is a group scene, is the major char-acter in a clear enough area to do his acting? Does the scene require a close-up for him to punch his point home? Are the poses well-delineated?
- Does the scene shift in importance from one character to another? Is it com-posed to account for this shift in importance? Can the secondary characters add, through movement, importance to this shift through head turns, changes of posture, reactions to what is being said, etc.?
- Has *continuity* of characters from scene to scene (which ones are included, their postures and movements) been accounted for? Is there continuity from scene

to scene of the character's relationship to the BG? (If a character is standing in front of a door in the medium shot, is a piece of the door and its relationship to the character shown in the close-up?)

- Leading the audience's eye in a two-character sequence:

Around a frame:

1st major movement – Norman walks in.	2nd major movement – Norman leans down to sniff.	3rd major movement – Gopher pops up during restricted sniffing movement.	4th major movement – Gopher rears back during continued sniffing.	5th major movement – Gopher kicks butt. Both move broadly.

From scene to scene:

As above	As above	Cut to C.U. as Gopher pops up, retaining piece of Norman as continuity.	Gopher rears back and kicks. Norman shifts in reaction.	Cut back out as Gopher comes out of kick and Norman is in mid-air.

Leading the audience's eye in a group shot:

Little mouse says, "Listen, fellers! The cat is our friend!" Other mice nod appreciatively.	Cynic mouse turns around in the opposite direction and snaps, "Ah, horse chestnuts!" Other mice turn to him in reaction.	Cut to medium C.U.: Cynic waits until he's sure all eyes are upon him.	Then he wheels around and says, "Cats is rats!!"

- Stage your characters as interesting compositional elements within the scene. Contrast tall and short, near and far, lit and shaded, etc.

Example: Hero is sad, Sidekick is sympathetic. Hero has the dialogue.

OK, but kind of boring profile.

Better, because it emphasizes Hero, and helps you feel more about what *he* is feeling. Also, by making Sidekick even smaller, he looks even more helpless.

Example: Slimeball is trying to force his charms upon unwilling Gal.

Dull

Better, because Slimeball's diagonal thrust contrasts Gal's straight vertical. Also better because Gal no longer is facing Slimeball — her physical refusal to listen makes him have to work harder and get closer!

■ Staging Your Characters in a Dialogue Scene

- Allow enough time for what one character is saying or doing to sink in to the other character's brain. Don't have the "listening" character react too soon or he'll step on the active character's performance.

• Don't break the 180° line when planning compositions or cuts.

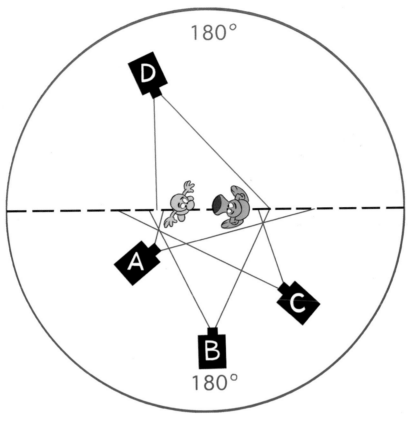

CAMERA Ⓐ OK

CAMERA Ⓑ OK

CAMERA Ⓒ OK

CAMERA Ⓓ N/G !!

Other more extreme but OK cuts might be:

   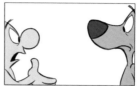 

The occasional off-screen reaction (someone listening to the main speaker) is nice, too, but remember to keep them facing in the right direction to the established relationship:

Right!   Wrong!   Best!

A little air on the left of screen is best: in the event you cut to a C.U. of the other guy, their body shapes won't overlap so much from cut to cut!

- Get value out of moving holds and traceback holds while the main character is emoting. Just because one person is talking doesn't mean the listener should be dead. He can still be doing an underplayed movement to show he is paying attention!

Plan your characters' actions so they overlap the cuts a little.

Shot 1: Hero's head turns toward Sidekick as he finishes his line.

Shot 2: Sidekick says his line, while Hero's head resolves up into a hold to watch.

▪ Staging Multiple Character Scenes

- What do you want your audience to see? If you're trying to highlight a particular character amongst a crowd, a few things might help: brighter colors on that character, a drifting camera move toward the character, other characters animated to reveal your lead character.

- Does the focus shift in the scene? Perhaps you want to start with one character walking through a scene amongst a crowd of people and you then want to pick up another character trying to follow him. Example:

Shot 1: Starts as dog walks toward screen right. Camera drifts in to pick up little puppy coming toward us.

Shot 2: Cut to puppy center screen while crowd and BG pass by.

- Can camera moves help you to lead the audience? Perhaps a gentle drift, if not an out-and-out truck-in, toward where you want the audience to look would be enough. Maybe your scene starts as an establishing shot with many characters as the camera moves toward the hero. Perhaps a character turns quickly and you whip-pan to what he sees.
- Are there actions that can be read as general activity in a multiple character shot? If the impression you want to convey is one of general hubbub, you can plan the scene for fairly contained movement without accents that are too strong, for two reasons:

  – No two viewers will necessarily settle on the same crowd character. Have a few minor accents to chew on but nothing too outrageous.

  – If you have your hero in the shot, you can then afford to give him more distinctive movement to draw the audience's attention.

■ Economy of Staging

- Find ways of making a two- or three-character situation into essentially one-character shots. Establish the situation, then use close-ups to focus in.
- Are there times an effect can tell the story?

Examples:

a. A cast shadow of a character against a wall and the other character watching.

b. A large portion of a character passing in front of a character farther back.

c. A change in lighting to tell the mood of the scene.

d. Characters in silhouette.

- Does the camera need to move? Can you tell the story effectively with simple cutting and composition? In other words, use the camera movement for specific storytelling reasons, not just for the sake of moving it.

Optional exercise: A little boy is wandering in a crowded city. He gets lost in the shuffle until he shouts, "Stop!" and the crowd freezes. He then asks the anxiously awaiting multitudes: "Where's the bathroom?" Stage the sequence in rough story-board form.

Timing

As everything is based on 24f = 1 sec., multiples of 4 are quite useful measuring guides (especially when pre-timing your X-sheets, as they are easy to mark off visually, as opposed to, say, 6's or 10's). Not everything you do will work out easily to 4 multiples, but there really isn't any reason to time on *odd* numerals (7's, 9's, etc.) unless you have a musical track whose beats drift plus or minus 1 frame or so. The difference between 7 frames and 8 frames is not enough for an audience to really perceive as a change in timing, but they would feel a difference between a run on 6's and a run on 8's.

Here is a rough guide for types of actions whose accents occur once every 2 frames, 4 frames, etc.:

2's – Staggers, vibrations, shivers, Woody Woodpecker pecking

4's – A fast run, a head shaking "no," an impatient foot tap

6's – A slightly slower run, a quick basketball dribble

8's – A "normal" run or a *fast* walk, tapping foot to music, hammering a nail

10's – Jogging pace, a quicker than normal walk (especially useful for short-legged characters)

12's – A "normal" walk or march step, a run in which funny "up" keys are accented

16's – A deliberate walk step, in which the elaboration into and out of keys is more florid (an "attitude" walk)

18's to 24's – A tired character's drag-footed slog, a sneak.

The shortest amount of screen time for a hold or a moving hold to register is 6 frames. (Anything less tends to look like a camera error or the interruption of an action.) 12 frames is about enough for a facial expression to register, 16 frames is stronger if you have the screen time, 24 frames is often too long (unless the expression is one of stealth or something that similarly is more fun as it unfolds, rather than quickly telegraphed). Certain actions look best with a slight pause in the middle, such as picking up a pencil, closing a book, knocking something over, etc., so that the point of contact can be "felt" by the audience.

T1

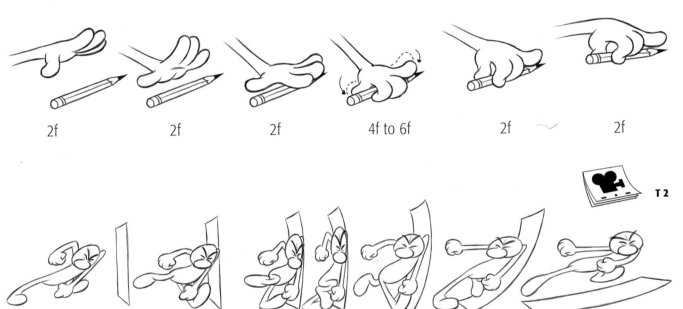

2f   2f   2f   4f to 6f   2f   2f

T2

1f   1f   2f   2f   1f   1f   1f

Sometimes the amount of screen time needed to show a particular movement can be very short, if what precedes and follows the movement is elaborated well enough (and for long enough):

T3

(Anticipation – 10f)   1f   1f   (Recoil on face and hat – 16f)

Avoid "twinning" in timing of arms and legs, as it tends to look unconvincing in all but a few areas.

Example:

Instead of raising the arms on exactly the same timings and cushions…,

Separating the arms by about four frames or so looks more fluid and natural.

This is a less fluid and convincing jump…

…than this, where one foot follows the other.

As well as varying the timing throughout a scene (building and altering rhythms, letting pacing within a scene reveal character-type), varied timing within a *character* can also be effective if handled properly. Basically, if you have two strong, resolved poses, you can advance and delay various body parts as they arrive at the final position, so long as these parts work organically and logically.

Example:

Cranium leads anticipation, nose tips up.

Head leads, right arm slides back.

Left arm lifts.

Head reaches apex, elbow contacts table as left hand is still following through.

Head goes down and contacts left hand (slight squash). Wrist breaks on right arm as it heads towards hip.

Head and left arm recoil back up as right arm finally settles in.

A word about quick timing—

A fast-paced cartoon like an Avery or a Clampett does *not* mean that everything occurs at breakneck speed. Most of the *transitions between* major poses or attitudes are very fast, but what comes before and after is still timed to be *readable*. The fact that things "snap" from one thought or extreme pose to another is what makes things funny, by occurring so quickly as to be unexpected. The audience, however, should always be able to perceive the "before" and "after," as opposed to animation that races through the storytelling poses as quickly as the inbetween phases. Check out the vulture in Clampett's *A Corny Concerto*, as he sees his prey, points to it, whips around with an "Out to Brunch" sign, and zips out of frame. All the poses are on *just* long enough to perceived, with those quick transitions on ones between them!

9

Spacing

Spacing, like timing, is something that you develop as a personal style after years of practice. After a while, timing and spacing will become *one* process during animation. As you become more adept, you will be able to time your inbetween charts with a pretty good knowledge of what your as-yet-undone inbetweens will be spaced like. A few basic principles:

- ## The more your drawings overlap, the smoother your action will look.

This doesn't mean that all your drawings should have the same degree of overlap, but that, for most of your actions, your drawings shouldn't be spaced so far apart as to "chatter." You'll notice this effect in certain animation scenes because the drawings are spaced too broadly for twos. If a part of your scene doesn't look fluid, go back and put single inbetweens in, and shoot the section on ones, thus making the degree of overlap between drawings similar to that on your more closely spaced twos. In other words, go through the scene and determine first which drawings are spaced close enough to remain on twos, and then only put the ones in where you feel the spacing between the drawings requires them. It saves work, and this back-and-forth working of ones and twos gives your animation texture and variety.

■ **The closer together your drawings are, the slower your action;
the farther apart they are, the faster.**

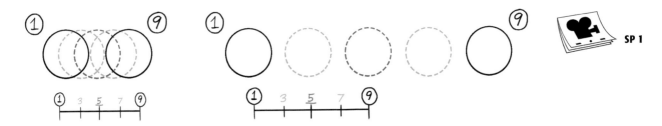

SP 1

Two sets of drawings above, timed the same way. The second set goes faster, because it's covering more than twice the distance as the first set in the same amount of screen time. (Note, too, that the second set could use single inbetweens, so the drawings will be overlapping.)

■ **Most normal actions can be thought of in terms of
acceleration → deceleration.**

Even if the spacing is quite wide in the middle of an action, if you prepare an audience to see the action (with cushion-outs, or an anticipation), do the action, and then follow it up with enough drawings for the eye to adjust (recoil or cushion-in), you give the audience the chance to "read" what has happened – even if the major part of the movement has occurred quickly.

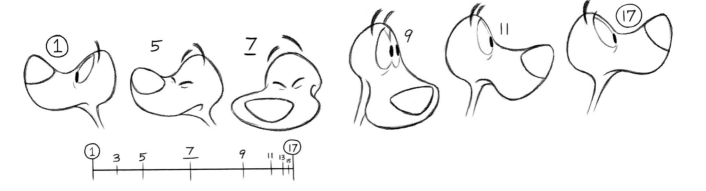

■ The Inbetween Chart

This is used to indicate the specific drawing numbers of key poses, breakdowns, and inbetweens, and the order in which they should be drawn. The charts should be written on the key drawings in the scene. A typical inbetween chart, with the keys circled and the breakdown underlined, for an action that cushions-out from 1 and cushions-in to 17, exposed on twos, would look like this:

From this, you can see that the two keys are ① and ⑰, and that the breakdown **9** is to be drawn first between the two keys. 7 then is drawn halfway between 1 and **9**, 5 is drawn halfway between ① and 7, and 3 is drawn halfway between ① and 5. Likewise on the other side of the chart, 11 is drawn halfway between **9** and ⑰, 13 is drawn halfway between 11 and ⑰, and 15 is drawn halfway between 13 and ⑰.

It should be noted, however, that a lot of variation and eccentricity can be utilized on the breakdowns and inbetweens, so that the animation has some life and personality to it, instead of just a mechanical parsing of phases out of or into a pose.

You might also encounter vertical charts, which look like this:

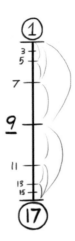

The only reason I do them horizontally is that when we animated commercials at Richard Williams Studios in the 70's and 80's we drew directly on cel with grease pencil, camera-ready. Thus, the horizontal chart was drawn between the pegs, outside of camera range. Ah, memories....

Very occasionally, "thirds" might be required on a chart to give an action some snap:

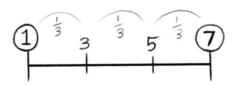

My recommendation is to use these as little as possible, as it is more difficult for clean-up artists or inbetweeners to interpret. Moreover, I generally consider these "eccentric" drawings that should be drawn by the animator and not left to chance. At the very least, do one of the thirds (say, 3); then the remaining drawing, 5, becomes a halfway between 3 and ⑦.

You can also space your drawings for added fluidity, by conceiving your charts for both ones and twos simultaneously:

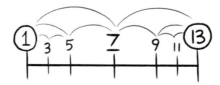

The chart above, from ① to ⑬ , would be your average cushion-out cushion-in on twos.

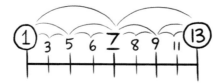

If you decided to put ones in the middle of the move for smoother action, it would help, but your spacing would then wind up equidistant, and there would be an unnatural speed-up of the singles on screen.

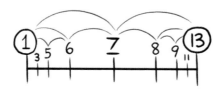

Instead, try conceiving your chart like this, where 6 is halfway between ① and **7**, and 8 is halfway between **7** and ⑬. It's exactly the same number of drawings, but now there is a more convincing acceleration and deceleration that you can see clearly on the chart, even before you execute the drawings!

■ The gap between the drawings!

To give your work some snap, you can work the gap between drawings so that the movement has more impact. By using the idea of preparing an audience for an action and then following it up with convincing cushions or reactions, you can leave a huge, non-overlapping gap between drawings, which will work fine for "impactful" actions.

Particularly useful for:

Throwing a punch –

SP 2

Doing a take –

SP 3

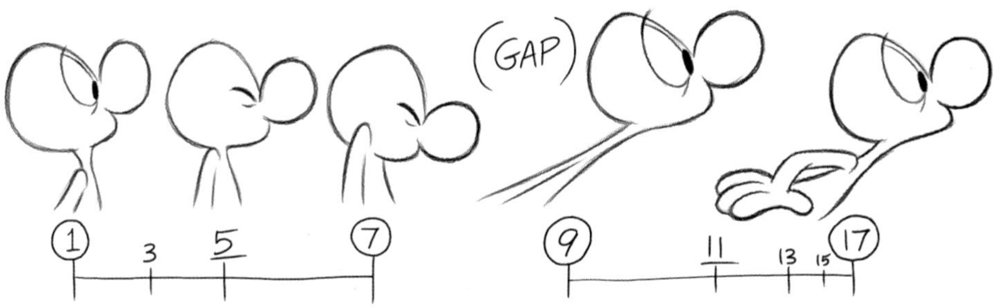

Swatting a fly –

SP 4

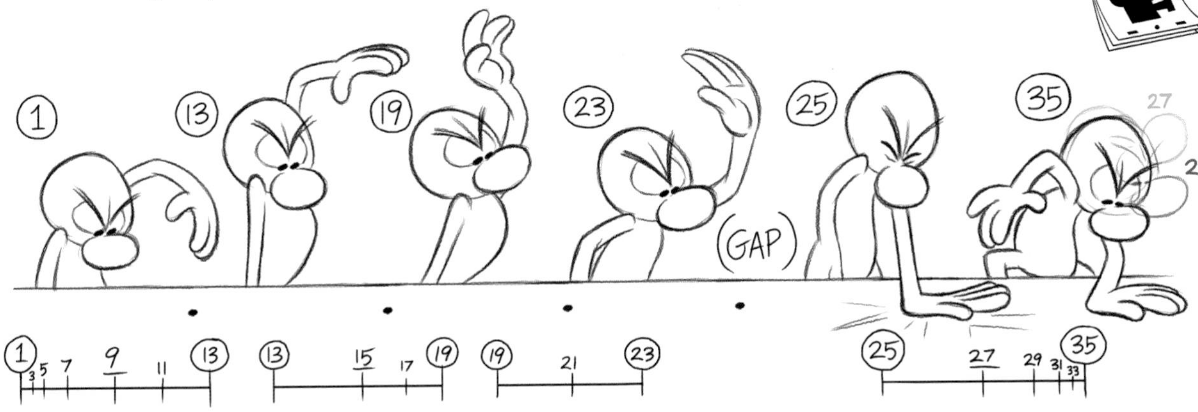

Fainting —

SP 5

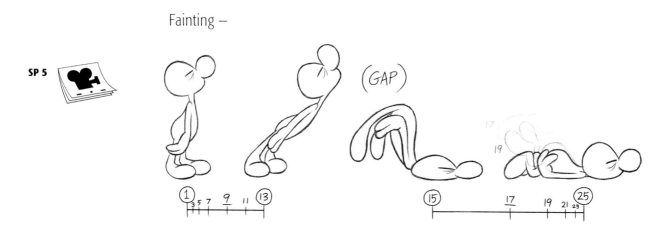

A nice variant on the preceding is to go from a hold (or a moving hold) with no anticipation or cushion-out, and then cushion-in to the following pose. (I learned this one from Gerry Chiniquy, the great Yosemite Sam animator, on a "take" scene in *Raggedy Ann & Andy* !)

SP 6

Bear in mind that all of the above "gap-working" is to be used *sparingly*, only when needed. If used constantly, your work will klunk around jerkily and give your audience a headache. (Yes, I know, several of you reading this are going, "But that's what I want!")

Spacing in CG Animation

Because a computer is capable of creating accurate inbetween positions, and they don't have to be hand-drawn, the tendency is for most CG animation to be on ones, all the time. This poses some unique problems, since a uniform usage of ones in both hand-drawn and CG often results in floaty, evenly spaced action. Hand-drawn has the edge here, since the working of ones and twos is commonplace; CG animators have to work harder to give their work punch and poses that telegraph strongly, since the automatic ones can even things out. This means that, in CG, a gap may need to be exaggerated, or a "favored" inbetween even closer to the source key, in order to give the same effect one would get in the hand-drawn world. There are also instances where CG animation can be twos, most notably when it is blended with hand-drawn animation on twos in the same scene. In *Pocahontas*, Grandmother Willow's facial animation on twos is blended with her outer CG bark, also on twos, so that the two marry together in the frame.

10

Having a Breakdown!

After establishing your pose drawings for a scene, roughly time them on the X-sheets. (Number the sheets all the way down on odd numbers on twos: 1, 3, 5, 7, etc., and number your pose drawings as to their approximate placement for timing.) Then work out the charts for your breakdowns (BDs) and inbetweens. The thing to bear in mind is that the breakdown drawing you make can contain practically all the necessary information for overlap, delay of different parts, personality, etc., so that the remaining drawings are almost straight, dead-in-the-middle inbetweens. When I was working at Richard Williams Studio in London, Ken Harris was there animating on *The Thief and the Cobbler*. At 80 years old, he could turn out 30 feet a week of gorgeous animation. I was astounded, and asked Ken how he did it. Ken's reply was a self-effacing, "Aw hell, I can't draw, it's all Dick's poses," etc., etc. So I did the next best thing and asked Dick how he did it. Dick's reply: "Well, Ken's a master of the charts," and he patiently explained to me that Ken's ability to place the breakdown in exactly the right position, and then chart a cushion-out, cushion-in, gave his animation automatic overlap when the rest of the inbetweens were completed. It is the single-most important lesson I ever learned in this medium, and it opened my eyes to how animation could be *planned* for ease of execution and maximum effectiveness.

Example:

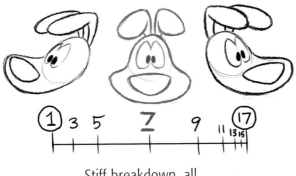

 BD 1

Stiff breakdown, all
parts moving at the
same time.

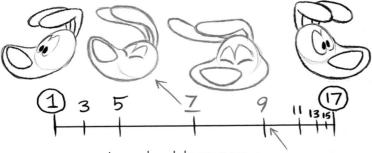

 BD 2

Loose breakdown: nose
up, cranium down,
drag on the ears, favor-
ing the first key

Your next inbetween could
also be a "breakdown" of
sorts, following the flow and
leading into the cushion
drawings.

The breakdown drawing is what can add interest to a basic movement: whatever arcs, delays, paths of action are in the BD are reflected in the entire move. In other words, why go A→B→C, when you can go A↘F↗C?

If you want drag on an arm movement, the breakdown can do it for you!

BD 3

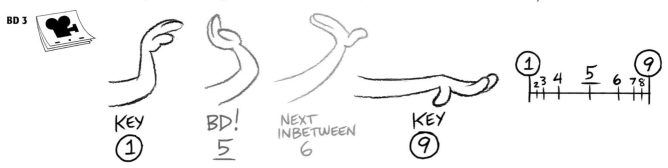

A simple head lift can get automatic overlap by placing the BD askew:

BD 4

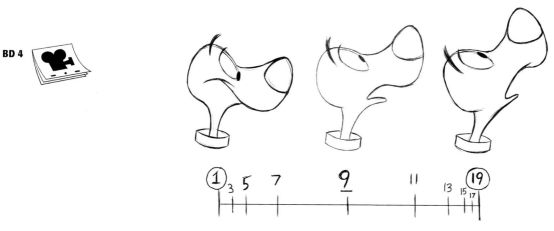

Instead of a dead center breakdown, which would give you a smooth but uninteresting action…

BD 5

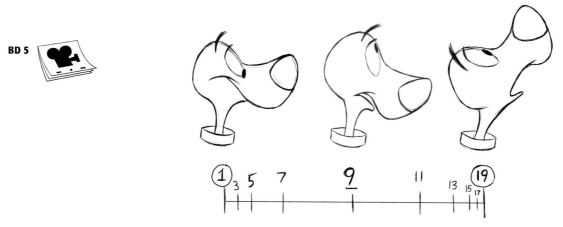

…throw the BD askew and get free drag and overlap!

Basically, the spacing on your charts serves as a rough guide to what's a cushion and what isn't, but how you make the BD drawings isn't necessarily a *dead-in-the-middle*, mechanical process. By working the BD, your movement can have snap, overlap, and heretofore unseen shades of personality.

Here are a few examples that show how a different BD between identical keys can thoroughly change the behavior and movement of the character:

The crouched position on BD 9 gives a feeling of cautiousness.

The arced BD here, with everything supporting his gaze, makes him more curious.

The exaggerated straights and the head overshoot on this BD make it a "shock take."

Same charts, same timing, totally different actions. In short, if the key poses are *what* the character is doing, then the breakdowns are *how* the character does it. (Remember, this stuff is all in pursuit of the *performance*, not just to make it interesting!) On the movie tests of these scenes, I've deliberately not added any bells and whistles (drag, overlap, delayed timings on arms). The inbetweens are just that – dead-in-the-middle accurate – so it's clear how the one BD drawing can affect the entire flavor of the movement.

Breakdowns in walks:

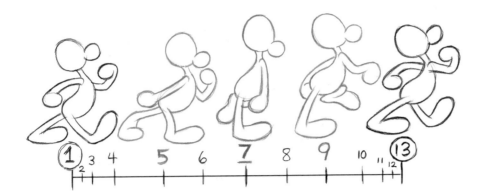

BD 9

If you key your down positions ① and ⑬, and your passing position is your major breakdown **7**, then the secondary BDs **5** and **9** fall between, giving drag and weight. On 5, the head goes down, the right arm straightens as it passes through, the left elbow goes out and down, while the fist rotates slightly. The left foot favors the key, while the right foot has snapped down. On 9, the nose continues to follow through, while the cranium (favoring the passing position) starts down. The torso continues its upward move as the right foot is at its most stretched. When the rest of the inbetweens go in, they can be practically dead-middle types, as all the drag and follow-through has already been taken care of on the BDs.

Breakdowns for eccentric action:

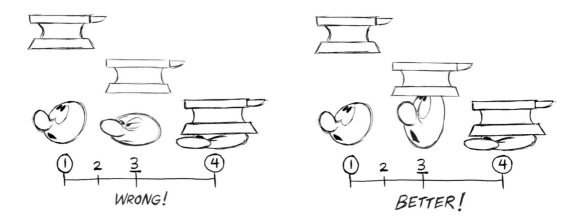

Obviously, 3 shouldn't be a halfway drawing, even though the spacing chart is right for the anvil. By leaving the chart to be applied to the anvil, you can progress the character's expression so that the squash can have even more impact when it comes. One time at Richard Williams we were single-framing some Charlie Chaplin, in a sequence where he was drunkenly attempting to cope with a swinging clock pendulum. We were surprised to discover that Chaplin was such a good mime that he could throw his head forward for one frame before throwing it backward to register taking it on the chin from the pendulum, in order to heighten the impact.

11

Squash and Stretch

One of the most basic patterns of movement used to show squash and stretch in animation is that of the ubiquitous bouncing ball.

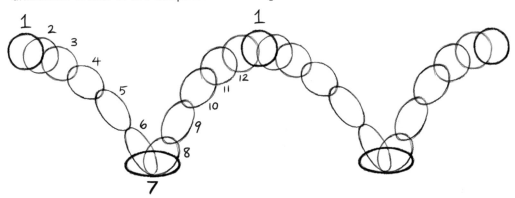

The above pattern shows the standard way to animate a bouncing rubber ball – it's caricatured, but based on the physics of what actually happens in reality:

Drawing 1 – The ball in midair, at the top of its arc, in its most spherical shape.

Drawings 2 & 3 – Gravity starts to pull the ball downward in an arc. The drawings are still fairly close together.

Drawings 4, 5 & 6 – The ball stars to elongate, as the acceleration increases. The spacing gets progressively farther apart. Note that on #6, the ball, elongated, is touching the ground. This is so the audience can register the shape change as a "squash" because 6 and 7 overlap.

Drawing 7 – The ball continues making contact with the ground and squashes.

Drawings 8, 9, & 10 – The ball shoots upward toward the top of the next arc, stretching out, with drawings spaced far apart.

Drawings 11, 12 & 1 – The ball slows down and becomes spherical again, as it arrives at the top of the next arc. The drawings are spaced closer together as they progress back to #1.

Not only does this demonstrate "squash and stretch" principles, but also the spacing principle that the closer the drawings are together, the slower an object moves, and the farther apart the drawings, the faster it moves.

Innumerable applications of "squash and stretch" are used in animation to make characters look more alive and fluid.

Squash and stretch in a jumping character.

Squash and stretch in a facial "take."

"B ———————— OO ——————— oo!"

Squash and stretch in dialogue.

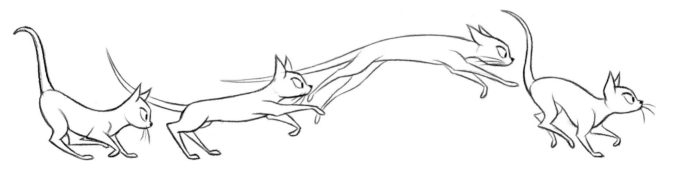

Squash and stretch in an animal run.

Sometimes it's useful to think of squash and stretch as an expanding and contracting accordion: one end moves first, the accordion stretches out, then the other end catches up.

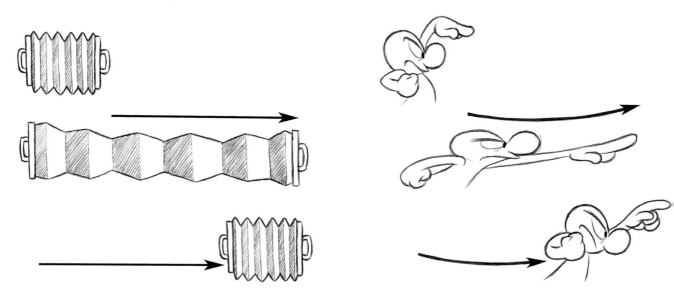

However, unlike an accordion, when an organic character squashes and stretches, his parts should maintain the same volume as they would in normal actions. In other words, don't just contract and elongate, mush up and displace on squashes, and skinny out on stretches.

SS 1

WRONG!   RIGHT!

Of course, don't forget squash and stretch when a character meets an immovable
force!

12

Overlapping Action

Overlapping action is the principle that not everything in or on a character arrives at the same time. This can be applied broadly or subtly, but ignoring it altogether will probably give you stiffer animation than you would want in all but the most subtle and slow of actions.

■ Conceiving overlap from pose to pose

Instead of making poses that work only mechanically, attempt to convey a sense of constant life and "give" in every character you draw: that some parts go first, and others drag behind and catch up later.

This first group will work all right, but will be dull and stiff.

This second group will do the same thing, but with much more life and feeling of plasticity in the forms.

Granted, not everything you will be required to animate will be suited to this kind of treatment in the drawings, but even in the most "straight" pieces, the notion that the characters have a sense of "give" when you draw them adds zest to your movement.

■ Overlap on body actions

Animate different timings of body parts in the same move: don't have everything arrive at once, and avoid "twinning" of arms and legs unless for a specific effect.

Don't just inbetween something settling into position...

... break it up into parts arriving differently.

Avoid "twinning," both arms moving at the same time, like a mirror image.

Rather, separate the timing and positioning of the arms for overlap.

■ The Flapping Flag:

Like the bouncing ball as the shopworn demonstrator of "squash and stretch," the flapping flag is the industry poster child for overlapping action. When the stick is waved, that's the primary action, and the flag material attached to it is the secondary action that follows along behind it. When the stick changes direction, the flag catches up and overlaps before it too goes in the same direction.

■ Drag on hair and drapery

Hair — Have it lag naturally behind the movement of the head, and then settle with some "lilt" and bounce. This action of going past the final point of arrival and then settling back is called "recoil."

Drapery and clothing — How much drag (and also how much the material goes past and recoils) depends on how thick and heavy the material is. The thinner the material, the broader the overlap:

Thin waistcoat material

Heavy winter coat

■ Overlap on head movements and within facial detail

Don't be afraid to throw your head breakdowns askew (for example, leading with the cranium and delaying on the muzzle) to achieve overlap when the inbetweens go in:

Instead of this —   Try this!

Animate "give" in jowls, lips, brows, eye shapes, etc., without getting too rubbery in the cranium.

■ "Mini-smears" and when to make a bad drawing

Although your animation should work correctly, occasionally body parts, faces, and clothing can benefit from a distorted drawing that looks odd in hand but not in movement.

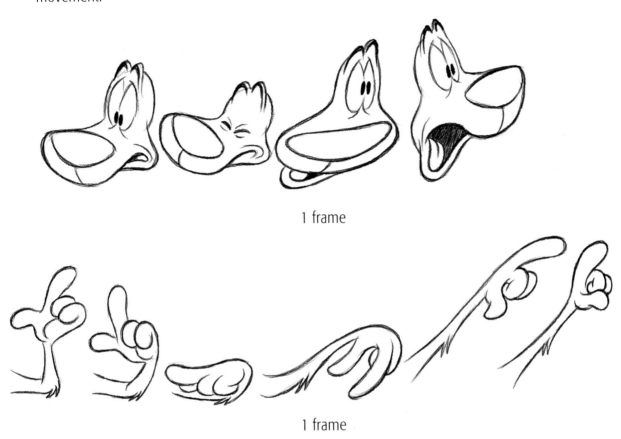

1 frame

1 frame

I call this a "mini-smear," meaning that it is the reduced version of a "smear" drawing (see "Gimmicks" chapter) that does the same thing on a smaller scale — it helps define an arc or add fluidity without regard to retaining volume as per a "squash and stretch." This kind of distortion almost always looks best for one frame only. (When on twos, people can perceive the gloopy movement instead of a quick blur effect.) Best version of this I've ever seen: Ken Harris' animation of Bugs Bunny's whiskbroom (on leftover crumbs of beauty clay) in *Rabbit of Seville*. More of this stuff later.

Optional exercise: Animate a run cycle. Then on a separate level animate:

Ears and
tail (bushy
variety)

Top hat and tails
(dinner jacket
variety)

13

Weight, Balance, Mass and Volume

Weight

Your characters are subject to the laws of gravity all the time (unless you are specifically breaking them for the sake of a gag). So, they should have a certain solidity on the ground, which gives them physical readability to the audience. A lot of this can come from thorough understanding of character construction, but should also come from indications in the animation that the character has weight.

- Overlap! Indications of drag on the character's head, belly, feet, arms, etc., show that the character must expend a certain amount of energy shifting himself (or a limb, for example) from one spot to another. How *much* to show is a matter of personal taste and adaptation to suit the particular character, but, basically, the faster the move, the more extreme the overlap can be.

Example:

W 1

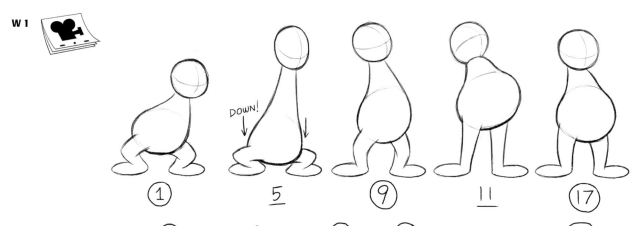

The above sequence of overlap and recoil would look about right if timed as the numbering indicates, and shot on twos. However, if you put inbetweens in after that, giving the character twice the screen time for the move, he'd look like a human waterbed. The same ideas apply to recoil as well as drag: enough to show natural settling, depending on the speed of the move, but not too much to make your character look jelly-like!

- Timing – Bearing gravity in mind, the bulkier your character, the more time his bulk should spend closer to the ground! In other words, the recoil should take less time than the drag and the settling to register heaviness. If you look at the above example, the belly is in a "down" on ①, 3, **5**, 7, 15 and ⑰, leaving only ⑨, **11** and 13 to register the recoil.

Also, if a character goes from "up" to a "down," if he accelerates out from the "up" quickly, hits the down, and recoils up, the weight will be registered more forcefully. This is particularly useful in a heavy-footed walk, or a stomp.

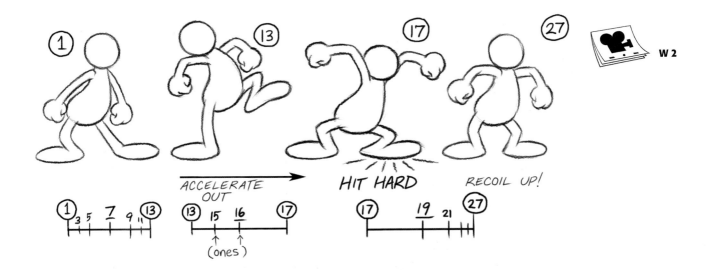

Generally, the heavier a character, the slower he'll move; the lighter he is, the quicker and more agile his movements. And if you have a heavy character who must move quickly, make sure to:

- Keep it sculptural.
- Give it overlap — but not too much time on the recoils: the bulk should stay closer to the ground most of the time. (Preston Blair's Fantasia Hippos are a good example of this.)
- Make sure contacts with the ground are hit hard.

- Anticipation — Almost any move looks more convincing with a bit of anticipation, even if it's just four frames or so, because it gives the audience the impression that the character needs to *prepare* himself to expend the effort to shift his own weight. Obviously, anticipation is also of prime importance when a character is shifting an external weight.

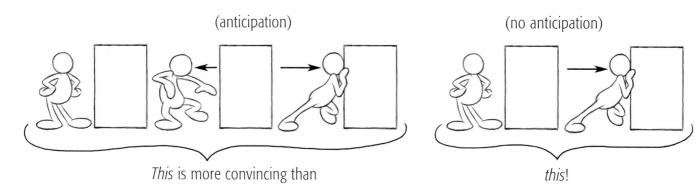

(anticipation)   (no anticipation)

This is more convincing than   *this*!

- Bodily shifts of weight — Changes in posture that show, for example, weight spread evenly across two legs, to weight taken more on one leg than another:

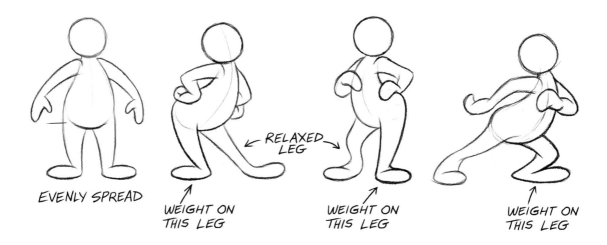

EVENLY SPREAD

WEIGHT ON THIS LEG

←RELAXED LEG→

WEIGHT ON THIS LEG

WEIGHT ON THIS LEG

Balance

The above examples show too that a shift in emphasis in weight must maintain balance. Balance is important in movement, too, because the pull of gravity dictates that an awkward passing position cannot take too much screen time (or the character will look like he should fall over) before his weight is adequately supported again.

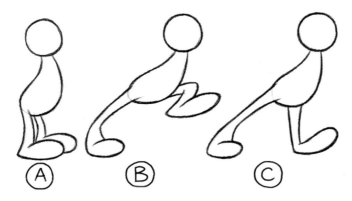

You can spend a little time getting from A to B, cushioning out, but C must follow B as the next drawing, because the midair leg in B can't be maintained without the character falling over!

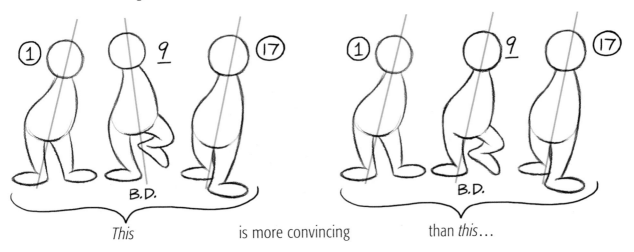

because the first set has a breakdown that maintains balance and takes more of the weight on one leg, while the second set has a weak breakdown, where the body does nothing to maintain balance and is a virtual inbetween between the two keys, other than the leg lifting. (It might work if timed faster but it's still unconvincing in terms of weight support.)

Mass and volume

Your character's construction determines his *mass*, his characteristic body shapes and features, which must be maintained in your animation as it moves in three-dimensional space. Look at the design of your character and note his salient physical features. Then devise ways that show these features to best advantage when the character moves. Does the character have a long nose, pointy ears, flat feet, potbelly, etc.? Does he look better in a ¾ view than front-face?

Example: A long-nosed character turns his head:

This works . . .   but *this* works better.

because it hasn't shortened and lengthened the nose in one move, it has shown the nose to remain long throughout the move. Note in both cases the foreshortening on "B," where the nose widens and flattens out to make it three-dimensional.

Foreshortening is quite important in every area of body movement, even on small features:

Turning a knee and foot   Turning a pointing finger   Looking up

Don't give your character a profile that is not believable for a more-often-seen front- or ¾-view:

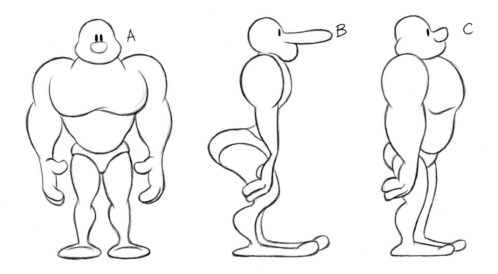

You *could* convincingly animate from A to B, but C works better for the audience because it's not a shock every time he turns around!

Your character's *volume* is the amount of space he would consistently take up, regardless of distortions or unusual positions. When animating distortions (a stretch or a squash on a character), make sure that they retain the same amount of volume:

Not this!	This!
Body just contracts or lengthens without regard to the amount of space it takes up when not distorted.	Body squashes out or elongates without shrinking or growing. The "take" drawing "skinnies-out" so he retains the same volume.

14

Properties of Matter

Throughout your animating careers, you will be required to animate objects and matter in relation to your characters. It will be necessary to convey weights, volumes, textures, densities, and recognizable behaviors for this matter, especially in contrast to the behavior of your character. Although much of this type of work is often handled by expert effects animators, character animators should know the principles too, especially for productions that may not have the luxury of time and a big budget. A few guidelines:

- **Think about weight and density first.** How light or heavy is the matter? Is it being dropped, carried, hurled, placed? Is it heavier on one end than another (like a shovel, or a baseball bat)? How densely packed are its molecules? Is it like an iron anvil, a piece of wood, some styrofoam? Does it have any "give" in movement, like drapery or a lump of mashed potatoes, or is it solid at all times? Is it something flexible that contains other matter, like a partially filled bean bag, or something hard that contains something flexible, like a bucket of water?

- **Don't rubberize unless you're animating rubber!** I can't begin to count the number of squishy anvils, baseball bats, sticks of TNT, cannonballs, and iron safes I've seen! Distortion on objects, like smear drawings or impact drawings, is OK in its correct usage, but rubberizing an object to make its movement more "fluid" when it's supposed to be hard and solid is just cornball cliché stuff.

- **Use timing and spacing creatively to convey different properties.** Besides good solid draftsmanship, timing and spacing will say as much about the matter (or *more*). Does it accelerate or decelerate in movement? Does it meet air resistance or cut through? Does the major move happen quickly while the secondary or follow-through movement occurs more slowly?

- **How does the matter affect the other matter around it?** Is the matter made of stronger or weaker material than that which it contacts? (Example: A heavy barbell dropped through a wooden floor could break through; dropped on a concrete floor it could bounce!) How much "give" would a character have if the object contacts him? Does the matter alter the matter it contacts? (Water spilled on a gray suit will darken it and maybe make it sag or stick to the character. Water spilled on a polished desk will just lie on top.)

Basically, the heavier and more densely packed an object is, the less you will be able to distort in your animation and have it look convincing. When a heavy object is dropped, the acceleration will increase more dramatically than in a lighter object, and the hit needn't be accompanied by a squishy drawing and cushioning.

PM 1

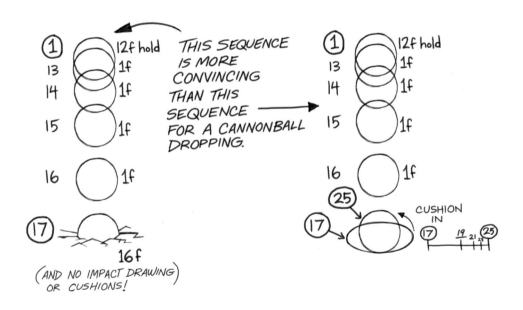

The second sequence works in a cartoony, cornball fashion, but doesn't convey weight and solidity nearly as much as the first sequence. (Note, too, in the first one, it's the *ground* that gives and not the ball.)

You can also convey flexibility without distortion in a solid object by animating an interesting pattern of movement and turning the object around three-dimensionally in the process. For example, if a character is getting beaned with a brick, the hit can be registered without distorting the brick (although you might want some distortion in the victim, thus making the brick appear even harder). After the brick makes contact, it can flip around three-dimensionally and land on the ground with a bounce, no distortion required.

PM 2

When animating wood (planks, for instance) you can employ a little "give" because you would see this naturally in life (particularly in longer planks), although you can exaggerate it more in cartooning.

Water animation is a bit tricky; the thing to remember is *irregularity*. Very rarely will something hit the water at such a perfect vertical angle, and the water be so still, as to make an even pattern of a splash. Often handled best as straight-ahead animation (or every *other* drawing straight-ahead, with inbetweens going in for the second pass).

A splash looks more convincing if it starts fast and dissipates slowly. Aside from the arcing and shrinking of the water droplets, the break-up should be uneven, and the falling droplets should start making ringlets of their own, animating outwards as the droplets hit. The water is displaced from the center outwards, and as the stone travels farther downward, the "hole" it made is filled in with more water, causing a smaller, secondary splash.

The same principles apply to mud, although it is drawn more thickly and timed more slowly, so as to look heavier.

When animating gooey, gloppy, or sticky substances, slow timing and close inbetweens are essential! (Take a look at the dog food glop slowly slurping out of the tin in Brad Bird's "Family Dog" episode of *Amazing Stories.*) Obviously, there's lots of room for distortion and recoil on this type of animation, as long as it happens slowly enough to look yucky.

PM 3

A lump of mashed potatoes:

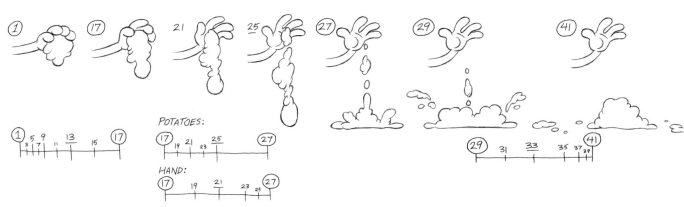

Paper, and other thin objects, like leaves, meet a lot of air resistance in movement, because they are so light.

Paper would never fall in an even, straight line, and when it hits the ground, it would slide a bit while settling.

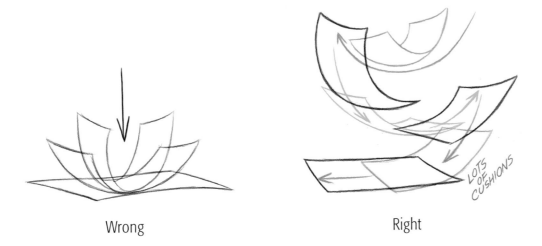

Wrong   Right

It is quite easy to overdo it with the overlap on this kind of animation; it's more important to retain recognizable shape combined with overlap.

Too much!   Better

Fire can be animated as a series of flickering shapes that grow, shrink, pop on, and break off.

However, unless animating a raging inferno, it's best to keep fire on twos and timed more slowly than it would occur in real life. This is because it is used almost always as a *secondary* action (in a fireplace, on the end of a stick, etc.) and would dominate the entire scene if animated too actively (dragons breathing fire notwithstanding). It's nice to build a gentle, undulating rhythm to the main body of the fire (and the inner color) while the top can afford to be more active.

Smoke and steam are best animated with a lot of inbetweens. If you animate straight ahead (on 8's, for example – one key every 8 frames) and then put 3 inbetweens between each 2 keys, your animation should have enough variation, but also enough slow pacing, to be convincing.

PM 4

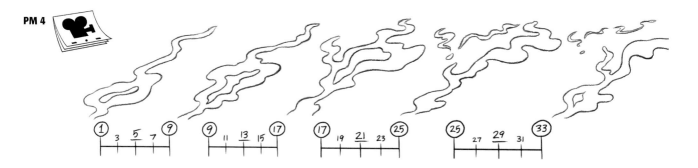

Think *varied patterns*, rising upward and gently dissipating. As in water, break-up should be uneven to look more natural, and it also looks better in animation for it to move more slowly (like fire) than it would in real life.

Drapery can be animated with flowing overlap and recoil, following the action of the character or object making the major movement. It's nice to show the underside of the material in your animation to give more three-dimensional form.

Thicker drapery (like a blanket, or heavy coat material) is animated in the same way, but timed slower, drawn with rounded edges, and conceived with more of a gravitational pull to show heaviness.

15

Facial Expressions

Usually, a common mistake in starting to draw facial expressions is to show the facial features as simple lines on the head:

Instead, think of a face as something three-dimensional, with forms that are "sculpted" on top of the basic head shape:

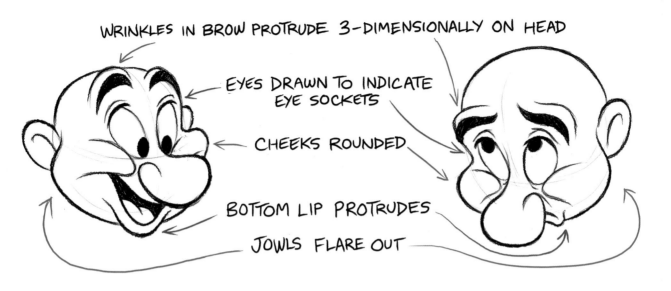

WRINKLES IN BROW PROTRUDE 3-DIMENSIONALLY ON HEAD

EYES DRAWN TO INDICATE EYE SOCKETS

CHEEKS ROUNDED

BOTTOM LIP PROTRUDES

JOWLS FLARE OUT

Once you're thinking like this, the next step is to imagine certain parts of the face as very flexible: eyebrows (and to some degree eye shapes), mouths, jowls, cheeks. Other parts would probably be less flexible (ears, nose, *cranium*):

Observe your own and other people's expressions and try to caricature them in your drawings – even if you're drawing "realistically" (say, the lead human in a Disney feature), the element of caricature is still important:

SMUG

HORROR-STRUCK

ANGRY

GLEEFUL

UNEASY

ALOOF

© Disney Enterprises, Inc.

As in animating dialogue, many animators like to use a mirror to act out their own facial expressions. (I think we've all seen the studio publicity photos of Norm Ferguson with his tongue sticking out while drawing Pluto and Ken Harris chomping on a carrot while drawing Bugs Bunny.) Others prefer to invent expressions based on observation, memory, and caricature. However you're comfortable working, *feel* the expressions as you do them – put yourself into your work and don't just rely on clichés from other cartoons.

Utilize elements on the head aside from facial muscles to make your expressions stronger – hair, glasses, hats, bowties, etc.

Here's a wolf with a derby   And the same wolf, angry –

Now, note how much stronger the expression is when we push the hat down on the brow, raise the cheeks, and flare out his side whiskers.

Also, don't forget how much stronger your facial expressions will be when supported by a body attitude that reflects the same thing:

16

Lip-Sync

Lip-sync is a particularly difficult area of the craft to master, since it needs to appear crisp for the sync to register, but not so exaggerated as to overpower the character's acting and expressions. Back in the late 1920's and early 1930's, when animation was just starting to require mouth movement, it was considered a miracle if the lip movements merely matched the primitive dialogue.

■ Garish 1930's style

We've all seen the various Fleischer, early Mickey, and Bosko cartoons that first flirted with lip-sync. As the young animators were trying to figure out which lip shapes corresponded with what sounds, they articulated each nuance with exacting detail and intensity. Unfortunately, this resulted in dialogue animation that gave every sound, whether quiet or loud, broad or subtle, equal visual importance on screen.

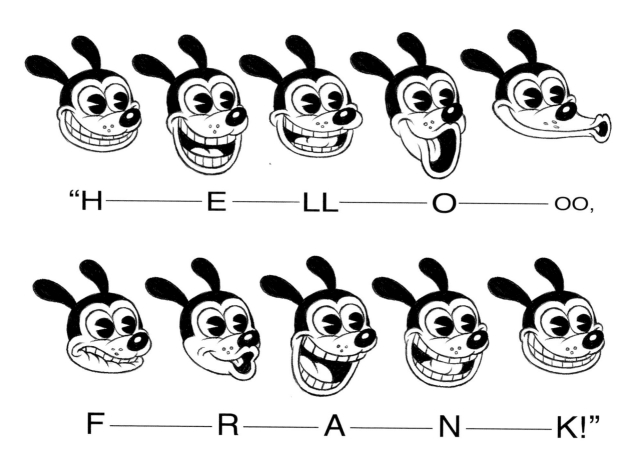

"H———E———LL———O———oo,

F———R———A———N———K!"

Granted, this has its old-world charm, but really isn't applicable to most lip-sync requirements these days.

■ The 40's Guys

In the great shorts animation of the 1940's and 50's, animators discovered not only that certain lip shapes should be broad while others remained more subtle, they also realized that head and body sync is more important than actual lip-sync. This is easily seen in your average Warners cartoon, where sometimes the dialogue articulation is a little mushy (they had to crank 'em out fast, folks!), but the head and body accents are so assured that the animation convinces anyway. The prime example of this is Marvin the Martian, who certainly convinces us that he is speaking, with nuance yet, but has no actual mouth! This is why the idea of phrasing was, and is, so important. When you start animating some dialogue, first listen to the track over and over, to find and memorize the proper accents and *dips*. (Dips are just as important, because the corresponding animation can reflect an anticipation prior to hitting a hard accent.) I say, "memorize," because you should know the nuances of the delivery well enough to imitate them yourself (!) so you don't have to keep stopping while animating to play the track again.

Give your animation light and shade in posing, but bear in mind that not every word or thought should have a separate pose. (Otherwise, your character will look like he's got ants in his pants.)

"DO — YOU — REALLY — THINK — SO?"

Ants-in-the pants version

"DO — YOU — REALLY — THINK — SO?"

Musical phrasing

Often one pose with an accent or two hit hard will suffice per sentence or thought. In the Freleng unit at Warner's, Gerry Chiniquy liked to animate dialogue with a lot of punch, often dispensing with inbetweens for his hardest accents (working that gap between the drawings!). Note in the example below (my poor rendition of a Chiniquy), that the hardest accents are not necessarily words but syllables, and an entire run of sounds ("What's the big i-") can be an anticipation before the next accent:

TH——AY!   WHAT'S THE BIG I—   DE—   A?

Obviously, it takes a certain bravura to be this punchy with dialogue, and it works better for more boisterous characters and situations than, say, Princess Aurora in *Sleeping Beauty*. (Although, now that I think about it, it *would* be kinda fun to see her animated like that just once!)

■ Broad or subtle? Teeth or no teeth?

In TV commercials, the graphic style utilized can frequently dictate what conventions to adopt for mouth shapes, and inclusion or exclusion of detail. Most cartoon characters with convincing lip-sync use mouth and tongue, but not teeth. You don't need teeth to make D, F, G, H, J, K, L, N, Q, R, S, T, V, X, Z, even though some animation books would have it that you do. Because of the type of exaggeration used in cartoon action, teeth often flash because they'll flap on and off as inconsistent areas of white (especially if animating on twos), so it's simpler to drop them altogether, unless teeth are an integral part of character (if he must grin or be supercilious or insincere – since he grinned a lot of the time, I did indeed use teeth on Aladdin's Genie). On *Raggedy Ann & Andy*, Tissa David gave the title characters certain rules: no blinks because their eyes are sewn-on buttons, and no tongue or teeth in dialogue, since they were cloth dolls with cloth faces. As her assistant animator, I learned for the first time how to manipulate mouth shapes alone for convincing lip-sync (thanks, Tissa!). In most cases, hard consonant sounds can be reduced to simpler shapes based on representations of what the mouth should be doing at the time:

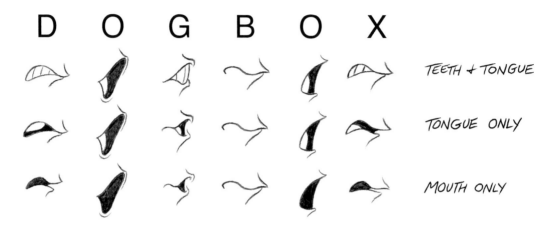

Whether you use broad or subtle accents depends on how naturalistically you want to portray the sounds (and can also depend on the type of character: is he bombastic, larger than life, timid, quiet, tall, short, nervous, cool?). Also, several characters in the same film shouldn't have the same mouth shapes; they should each have individual lip patterns unique to their personalities. A sterling example of great lip-sync (and accents) as well as great acting is Milt Kahl's masterful Shere Khan and Kaa "interrogation" scene from *The Jungle Book*. Note that Kahl only uses Shere Khan's teeth to indicate that he's got some in his mouth and they're dangerous-looking (particularly his bottom jaw), but not to grind every "D" or "G" he says. Instead the lip-sync is achieved through perfectly assured shape-manipulation of the mouth itself, aligned with equally assured head accents. Also, by using slight head turns and changes of angle, Kahl keeps the head and facial gestures in three dimensions (i.e., not all accents are up or down — they can be sideways, or tilting from one side to another).

■ The Nitty-Gritty

- When animating consonants, it's best to register them for 2 frames minimum. Even if the consonant is only on for 1 frame on the X-sheets, eat backwards into the preceding vowel for 1 frame extra to give 2 frames total. (This gives your eye time to register the closed mouth.) Only when the X-sheets go consonant, vowel, consonant, vowel, consonant, vowel for 1 frame apiece should the consonants only have 1 frame on the screen.

- Animate directly to the lip-sync on the X-sheets (don't precede the sound by 2 or 3 frames, etc.) unless you're on twos, in which case precede by 1 frame if a sound falls between your twos on the sheets. Never be a frame *late* on lip sync (or hitting musical beats, either) unless absolutely necessary. Keep in mind that it's always easier for the editor to slide a line of dialogue plus or minus a frame or two than it is to adjust to animation that doesn't correlate one-to-one with the sound. A lot of great Disney animators swore that head accents should arrive 4 frames earlier than the sound accents, but that the lip-sync should be bang on to the readings on the X-sheets. Warners' guys would usually hit head accents and sound accents at the same time. Having done both, I would say I prefer the latter, as it's punchier for cartoony characters. When animating on twos and then putting in single inbetweens, ensure that the consonants still hit for two frames and that vowel accents snap just as hard (i.e., make eccentric lip positions on the singles to maintain the same snap you would see if the animation remained on twos).

ON TWOS:

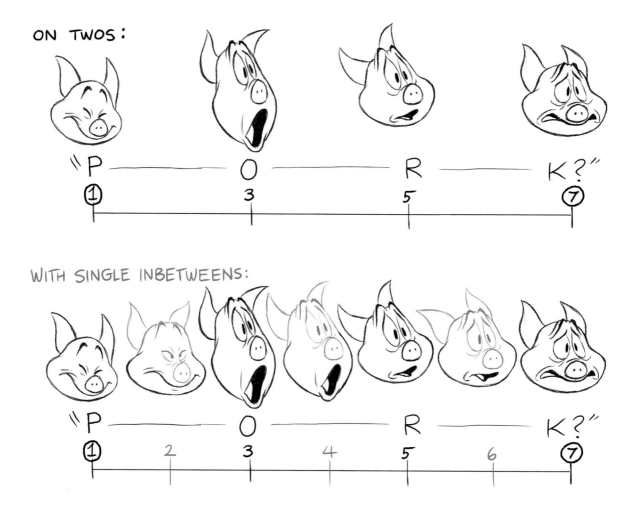

"P ————————— O ————— R ————— K?"
①   3   5   ⑦

WITH SINGLE INBETWEENS:

"P ————————— O ————— R ————— K?"
①   2   3   4   5   6   ⑦

- When animating vowels, hit the first drawing as the most extreme, then progress it to another position that "diminishes" the sound. This way, the vowel accents read clearly, but the diminishing animation cushions them. (Don't go from a consonant drawing to a weak vowel drawing, and then a wider vowel drawing — it'll look "backward.") Are there exceptions to this rule? Sure — I've noted a few in Milt Kahl's Shere Khan close-ups. In general, however, it's best to keep the lip-sync crisp in this manner. Also, for more subtle lip-sync, your "diminished" position can start to lead organically into the next key mouth position.

"DR —— O ———————— P!"

Wrong

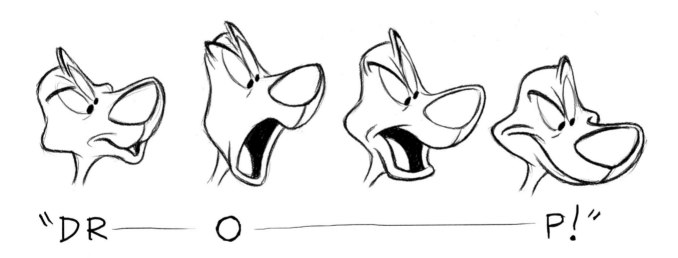

"DR —— O ———————— P!"

Right

- The mouth is *not* independent of the rest of the face. The mouth positions can (and usually should) affect the jowls, nose, cheeks, eyes, eyebrows, ears, even hair.

Consider all these things when animating. Overlap, squash and stretch, blinks, changes of expression all come into play. For realistic lip-sync, the same rules apply, but the accents are hit more subtly, and teeth are usually required. A great example is the caricatured CG lip-sync in *The Incredibles*.

- **Mouth shapes**

  Gear your mouth shapes to the type of character design you're using.

Don't give a guy like this –

a mouth like this –

when a more graphic handling would work better.

Or this guy –

this mouth –

when what he needs is three dimensions.

• Learn ways to hit sync when the mouth shapes are altered for expression:

HAPPY

S — I — T D — OW — N

SNOTTY

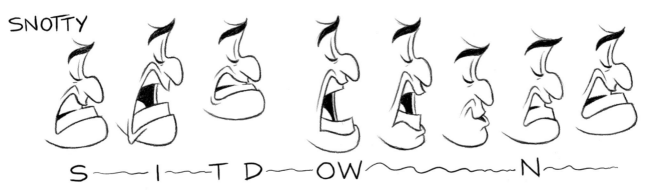

S — I — T D — OW — N

…and try to retain the same attitude through the lip sync, instead of one smile, one frown, one pucker, etc.

S — I — T D — OW — N

- Animating teeth – Always be sure to retain a portion of teeth showing whenever possible so they don't flash on and off. If you do drop them in the course of a line, bring them back again subtly over a couple of frames.
- Don't be tempted to animate just by looking at the sheets – listen to the subtleties of the delivery. (You may see a "D" on the sheets, but it might be silent or clipped in the actual take.) If a character says "last" on the sheets, is it "l*ah*st" like an upper-crust Brit, or a nasal "l*aaaa*st" like a New Yorker?

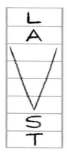

- Find out when you can be lazy with your lip-sync – use a mirror to determine how one sound leads naturally into the next without making the mouth shapes garishly distorted:

This one will pop and flash all over the place.

This one will look more natural, as one shape leads organically into the next.

- Don't be afraid to hit vowels hard — you can always lead in to them gracefully and then cushion up softly. Avoid mush!

- **A Word about CG lip-sync:** The big things to bear in mind are that your animation will always be on ones (so it's even more important to retain that snap for mouth shapes) and that CG has its own ways that work due to the fact that three dimensions, with light and shade, now can be considered as part of the vocabulary. My favorite example is the difference between a "P" in 2-D and 3-D. In hand-drawn, the "P" would usually be shown as a close-mouthed squash prior to the following vowel. In the CG *Toy Story*, they hit on a "P" that could show the upper lip puffing up three-dimensionally prior to the vowel. Both work great within their own contexts.

Optional exercise: Animate the same line three times, using:

A smiling
announcer

A scowling duck

A regal lion's
muzzle

Recommended Cartoons

Boop-Oop-A-Doop (Betty Boop / Fleischer) — Great over-articulated Fleischer lip-sync on Betty and friends.

Ain't That Ducky (Daffy / WB) — Punchy Gerry Chiniquy lip-sync in the Daffy cartoon with Victor Moore and the little yellow duck.

Hare-way to the Stars (Bugs, Marvin / WB) — Subtle Ken Harris dialogue on Marvin the Martian.

101 Dalmatians (Disney) — Caricatured but realistically believable dialogue animation by the masters, on Roger, Anita, Cruella, et al.

Toy Story (Disney / Pixar) — Love those "P" shapes, not to mention great acting and accent choices despite having to work with hard-bodied plastic characters.

The Incredibles (Disney / Pixar) — Animation Supervisor Tony Fucile (*The Iron Giant*) in 3-D! His hand is evident on the great lip positions in the dialogue.

17

Animating Shapes

Successful and fluid animation of shapes relies on the tricks hand-drawn animation can exploit in order to *keep masses consistent, regardless of reality!* In other words, just because something would occur in real-life one way doesn't mean that animators don't have the means to distort that physicality to get a smoother effect on screen. If you can think of your drawings as if they were already in *color*, it becomes easier to maintain masses, even if you must "cheat" to do so:

© Disney Enterprises, Inc.

This hand turn at the wrist will "flash" in color, because the hand is "thick, thin, thick, thin."

© Disney Enterprises, Inc.

This version, which "cheats" the flip-over, works *better* because masses are maintained in color!

Sometimes you'll find opportunities to describe an arc or an S-curve with your shape movement:

Tipping the head down and elongating the nose (a "mini-smear") helps describe the arc used to turn Phil's head.

This "swirl" on a head lift adds fluidity.

This beard turn is pretty stiff and boring.

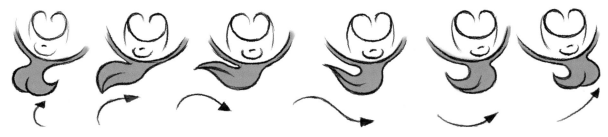

This "S-curve" beard flip is much more fluid.

This "S-curve" idea can be applied to a variety of shapes (such as hair, clothing) that require overlap. Below, the head moves forward, and the hair simply catches up.

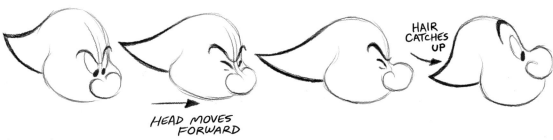

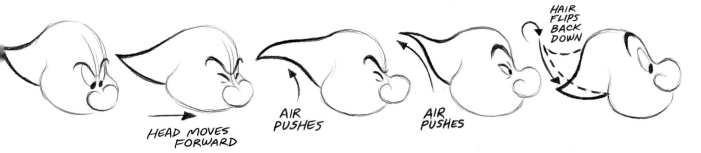

In the above version, the hair does an "S-curve," which is more fluid, because it takes air resistance into account.

You may encounter a scene that requires broad movement and quick timing. Getting into and out of the move gracefully makes your character "slick."

Although these shapes distort, they are all intended to support the "idea" of the action.

Sometimes distortions can acquire their *own* shape, which serves to amplify an action.

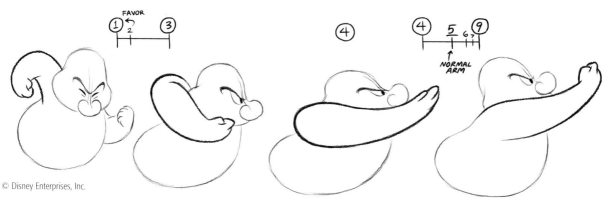

Retain some elbow as arm moves forward.

Into arc toward punch. Elbow shape starting to follow through.

Into punch and normal-looking arm.

The most distorted of these shapes should only be on screen for one frame apiece. Twos on this type of move would signal the "trick" to your audience. They would perceive the "gloopy" drawings when slowed down from ones to twos.

Show the audience that your characters can change shape!

This idea is really at the heart of spirited-looking character animation. By manipulating the shapes within a character, you convey the impression of constant life. It helps to underline emotional states as well, and uses animation's graphic qualities to make characters as expressive as possible. Say you have a character who is going to go from benign to furious. The stick figure version (and, alas, many CG versions) might look like this:

On the other hand, the cartoon version could look something like this:

By having the ability to show the shapes changing (the chest puffing up, the waist skinny-ing out), the cartoon version can be far more graphically expressive, using the entire body to telegraph the emotional state. Broadness aside, this type of handling is frequently a challenge in CG, where a modeled and rigged character, not unlike a stop-motion puppet, is frequently animated in layers (gross body movement first, appendages second, overlap third, etc.) that is counter to the more organic, but less anatomical, hand-drawn cartoon approach. It can certainly be achieved in CG, but frequently short schedules and restricted budgets tend to override the time-consuming effort it takes for this type of animation in the computer realm.

Flexible Drawing for Graphic Characters

Much of what you will be called upon to draw in your animation careers will have traditional construction and detail:

You can see that the above character has visible muscles, joints, bones, and a mop of hair that can be animated with traditional overlap. But what do you do when faced with a character like *this*?

How do you draw and animate a character like *this* without the result looking stiff?

The answer lies in convincing *shape manipulation*, whereby distortions are incorporated into the movement to indicate flexibility without "breaking" the graphic design. This way, an underlying anatomy can be *implied*: what still has hard textures and what has more "give" in movement.

Examples:

In a traditional head-turn, our doggie-friend might lead with his cranium. The muzzle might be looser and his hair and ears would overlap, including "breakup" on the hair:

Our graphic dog might turn his head like so:

Note the entire shape of head and muzzle becomes more flexible in Drawing 2. Also, the "hair" stretches but retains the graphic coils. Ears curve in the opposite direction. A slight indication of a bottom eyelid can come in when eyes are shut. In Drawing 3, more distortion and elongation is used on the muzzle and the eyes. The ears flip from a convex to concave curve to follow through, and the hair starts to arc through, still retaining coils. In Drawing 4, distortions are minimized as dog's face returns to recognizable graphic form. Coil hair follows through with a front view, which then springs past and settles.

You can apply these distortion techniques and disappearing/reappearing indications of anatomy to the entire body.

Example: Traditional dog lifts his leg (front leg, that is):

In the above, we use standard "breaking of joints" to show that, as the elbow rises, the wrist "breaks" to follow through. As the elbow falls, the wrist "breaks" again.

Graphic dog lifts his leg:

Graphic dog also employs "breaking of joints," the difference being that he forms an elbow and a shoulder when the movement requires it, and loses it when it is no longer necessary.

Shape distortion can be used on the whole body to give fluidity: just like standard "squash and stretch," except retaining graphic through-lines (the spine all the way up through the back of the head, for example).

What do you do when you have a character whose nose looks like a profile from a front view and you have to turn his head slowly?

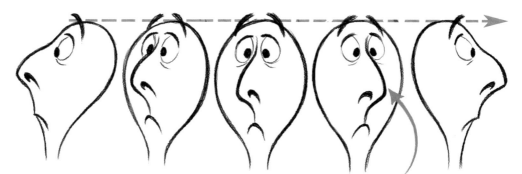

TO AVOID THE DREADED UNCONVINCING NOSE-FLIP, ANIMATE THE TURN WITH THE HEAD ON A DISPLACED ARC. THIS MINIMIZES THE "CHEAT" WHILE THE AUDIENCE REGISTERS THE LARGER HEAD MOVEMENT:

These and other "cheats" won't register as problems upon viewing if:

- The movement *through* the cheat is fairly quick.
- The beginning and end of a cheat movement have enough anticipation, cushion-out and cushion-in to make it believable.
- Secondary actions such as hair overlap, eye blinks, etc., draw your attention.
- The main movement is large enough or broad enough to hide the cheat.
- You hide the cheat on a drawing where another large action draws your eye — say a popped-open vowel on a mouth.

Animating to Music

Often animators are called upon to do musical animation, and are frequently given very little preparation or foreknowledge. ("Here's your scene, these are the beats.") I am not at all musically educated, but I knows it when I hears it, and I remain fascinated and inspired by the marriage of music and animation in films like *Fantasia*, the Warners shorts, and John and Faith Hubley's animation to jazz. This is a particularly difficult chapter to write without the benefit of audio-visual aid (i.e., video clips from cartoons and movies, the rights to which I would need to re-finance my house to license), but I encourage interested parties to seek out the various films referenced here, from both the classics and my more recent personal experiences, and see what I'm prattling about. So here, in no particular order, are some helpful tips and ideas:

- Hit your accents nice and hard! As in dialogue, if animating on twos, one frame ahead won't hurt the sync if the beat falls between the twos, but bear in mind this has a little trap: sometimes musical beats will fall oddly, say on 7's or 9's, and animating on twos just won't work. Also, whether we're talking about a 5-piece combo or an 86-piece orchestra, the marvel of human error means that not all the beats will be a consistent number of frames either – you may find that the beats in a run could go 8, 8, 7, 9, 8, 10, and your animation should work flexibly with it.

In this example X-sheet, the keys are circled for both animation on twos and animation on ones. Note that many of the "twos" keys fall a frame or two ahead of the beats, while the "ones" keys can be right on the money:

ACTION	KEYS ON TWOS		KEYS ON ONES
BEATS ✕	①		①
			2
	3		3
8			4
	5		5
			6
	7		7
			8
✕	⑨		⑨
			10
	11		11
8			12
	13		13
			14
	15		15
1			16
✕	⑰		⑰
			18
	19		19
7			20
	21		21
			22
			23
✕	㉓		㉔
	25		25
			26
	27		27
8			28
	29		29
			30
	㉛		31
2 ✕			㉜
	33		33
			34
	35		35
9			36
	37		37
			38
	㊴		39
			40
✕	41		㊶
			42
	43		43
7			44
	45		45
			46
	㊼		47
3 ✕			㊽
	49		49
			50
	51		51
8			52
	53		53
			54
	�55		55
✕			�56

- Be telegraphic with your posing and spend very little time *getting* to your pose – spend more time once you arrive (prime example: Freleng's hilarious Sylvester opus, *Back Alley Oproar*).

- Look at live-action choreography in movie and stage musicals. Often, body language is as stylized as a cartoon for maximum accent definition. (*On the Town* and *Singin' in the Rain* are fantastic treasure troves of information.) Watch conductors on the podium – Riccardo Muti, for example, literally hits key poses when he conducts! Ballets and modern-dance productions are also good research sources.

- Use one basic pose per musical phrase – not all the time, but it's surprising how snappy your animation can look through this kind of economy. Again, utilize quick transitions, and then spend more time once you've arrived at the pose.

- Vary the texture of rhythms and actions. (In the *Three Caballeros'* title song, the trio frequently shifts gears from wild scrambling to contained measures in Ward Kimball's boisterous handling.)

- Allow the audience the pleasure of seeing a repeated rhythm before you break away from it. Leave the repeated rhythm on screen for the full amount of time in the musical phrase whenever possible. In other words, if a measure has four beats, animate all four and then quickly transition to the next phrase and animate the next four, instead of breaking out of the phrase only two or three beats into the measure.

- Visualize your actions to follow the tone and pace of the music. Trying a long stretch and then a staccato movement for accent, for example, works well. In "Bumble Boogie" from Disney's *Melody Time*, the bee rattling the bars of his cage is perfectly conceived to complement the staccato piano run at the end of the musical phrases. The same piece also uses *color* change for musical heightening and accents.

- *Add* accents to your animation where you know a sound effect will work musically, even if it doesn't exist on the track. In the Genie's song, "Friend Like Me," I put in visual accents that would work when the sound effects went in, even though they weren't originally indicated on my guide track. When the Genie sings, "Some heavy ammunition in your camp," his rocket shape VOOMS over Abu and the

Magic Carpet, hitting a major (but not previously accented) beat. (In the final, it's fleshed-out with a great blare from the horn section!) When he spirals up singing, "And I'll say (BOOM), Mister Aladdin, sir," the explosion from wispy smoke to fully formed Genie accents the downbeat.

- Animating little musical stings at the end of a phrase can add humor and zest. In "One Last Hope," from Disney's *Hercules*, Phil uses his tail to brush the dust off a piece of buried statuary to complement the tiny musical sting provided by Alan Menken at the end of a particular phrase.

- Let your characters' movements be the musical accents, instead of relying on the scene cuts to do your work. Cutting works to a point, but accents *within* a scene work best – too much cutting can result in very fragmented screen rhythm.

- Beats and counterbeats – When animating a scene, you can use the main beats for one action while using the counterbeats and melodies for another. In *Rabbit of Seville*, Bugs is often animated to the insistent thump-thump-thump-thump of the beats for rhythm, while his hand flourishes are animated to the actual notes of the melody.

- When animating a group of characters to the same beats, don't animate all of them simultaneously to the exact same timings. Instead, offset some of their timings plus or minus a frame or two throughout the group, while others hit the beat right on the money. They will all still look as if they're in unison, but the variance from one to the next will make the animation appear more natural. The only time I wouldn't recommend this is when you really want the characters to humorously be in complete, exact, mechanical synchronization.

- **Know the musical structure.** This is really the big one, the Great Kahuna, the thing that really makes the animation and the music connect, and I didn't realize this until it was patiently shown to me on *Fantasia/2000*. Kent Holaday, an assistant animator by day, and expert sync-meister by night, showed me the musical structure on the Finale from *Carnival of the Animals*. He sat with me for two days doing this, before I even started storyboarding, and, through his enthusiastic love for both music and great sync, he gave me the tools I needed to conceive actions (and even determine the number of characters I needed) for the piece. For example, the structure for the opening measures, as the flamingos are out walking, goes: 1, 2, 3, 4 – trill – 1-2-3-4-5-6. Armed with this knowledge, I now knew I needed six flamingos, who would walk in lockstep for four steps (1, 2, 3, 4), leap and spin in the air (trill), and fall back down into the water (1-2-3-4-5-6).

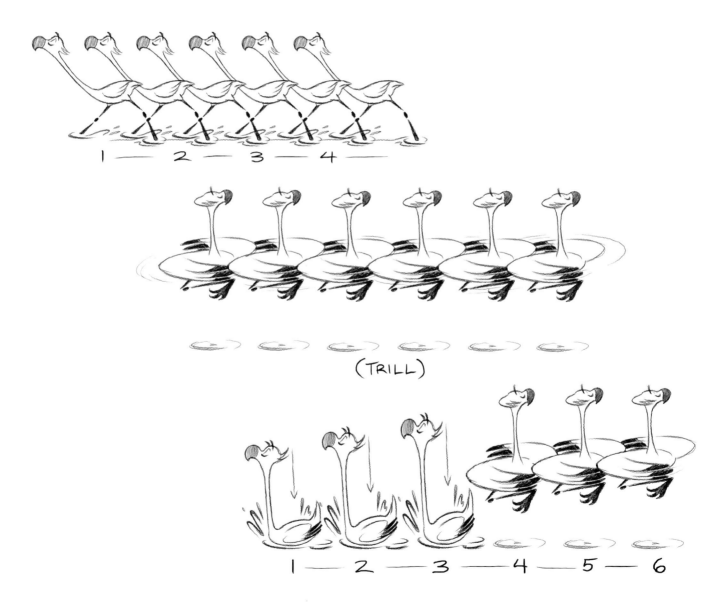

Kent showed me each time this structure was repeated throughout the piece, and I could see where the actions should be approached in similar fashion. He went through my entire set of X-sheets (for which he had personally read the music), showing me not only where the beats fell, but which instruments were playing, indicating visually on the sheets their individual rises and falls. He called this fabulous technique of his "Melody Timing," in honor of the musical Disney film. Naturally, when the time came to do *Rhapsody in Blue*, Kent was right there by my side again, this time topping himself by explaining to me exactly which fingers should be hitting which black or white piano keys in a sequence where I needed to animate Gershwin himself at the keyboard. (We had shot live-action reference of the pianist, Ralph Grierson, playing the piece, but whoever the cinematographer was that day managed to burn an electronic "Hello" over the image, right in the center of the screen!) In one scene animated by the great Andreas Deja, the beats are used to show the consistent steam whistle of the peanut wagon and the cranking of the street organ, while the piano countermelody is used for the monkey scrambling around stealing peanuts, all possible due to Kent's expert dissection of the different parts of the music. Sadly, Kent is no longer with us, but I know that his lessons will live on. Anytime I animate to music these days, I always think, "I wish Kent were here."

Gimmicks!

This is probably the chapter eager readers will turn to first, since it has all the fun goodies in it. (Oooh, look! An Irv Spence zip! A Chuck Jones smear drawing!)

Bear in mind, however, that the use of animation gimmicks is like the use of oregano in cooking – a little adds zest and spice; too much overpowers! Most of the following should be used *sparingly*, and in many cases not at all. The thing to remember is that they come in handy when there is no other way of physically expressing the action you want by animating "correctly." Sadly, they are more often used as a means of fudging a physically weak piece of animation (like blur lines every time a character moves his head or waves his arm – see Daffy's "Ducks going down in flames!" speech in the Art Davis *What Makes Daffy Duck*?).

"Blur" or "swish" lines — Used as a means to fabricate the look of a blur in live-action, or to support a "zip" with some "cartoony" flair. *Avoid* following the action exactly behind the blurs so the tail of Halley's Comet doesn't follow your animation around the frame.

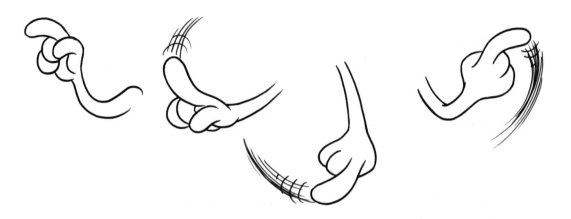

Wrong! This just looks like a tail!

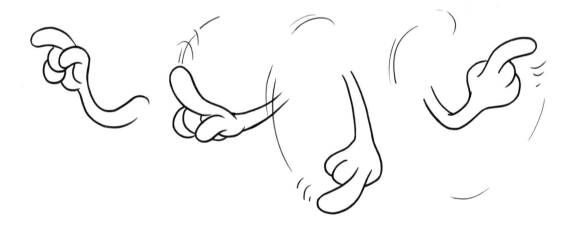

Better! The blurs (more lightly drawn) animate backward
from the movement and break up!

The "zip" also animates backward (and swirls inwards) while breaking up and dissipating. Irv Spence's Tom and Jerry zips are the best of this type.

G 1

When animating massive blurs (like the openings to Road Runner cartoons) make sure that your most intense darks follow through, to give the audience something to latch onto:

Back in the Golden Age, the success of blurs was largely dependent on the deft skills of the ink-and-paint department (mostly women be cause the male-centric animators claimed they had "steadier hands" – Glass Ceiling, anyone?). Their ability to "dry-brush" a blur onto a cel with the lightest of touches made the best ones look as if they had literally painted whirled air. Nowadays, with drawings scanned into the computer, the "dry-brush" effect can be duplicated by doing a softly rendered blur with pencil on paper, and scanning it as a grayscale. Once in the system, the blur can be further manipulated digitally to diffuse the edges, add color, and manipulate the opacity. I still miss the old way, though!

"Wiggle" lines when a character is supposed to be trembling or nervous are a holdover from comic strips. They rarely look good animated, as they do nothing more than form a "halo" without adding to the movement! Better to animate a convincing tremble instead. They *can* be used sometimes like blurs to follow an action:

Fooey!

Not quite as fooey, but almost.

A Convincing Tremble:

Step 1: Animate a smooth path on twos, with the correct overall timing. Key and inbetween as normal.

Step 2: Go back and put in eccentric inbetweens on ones for the parts you want to tremble.

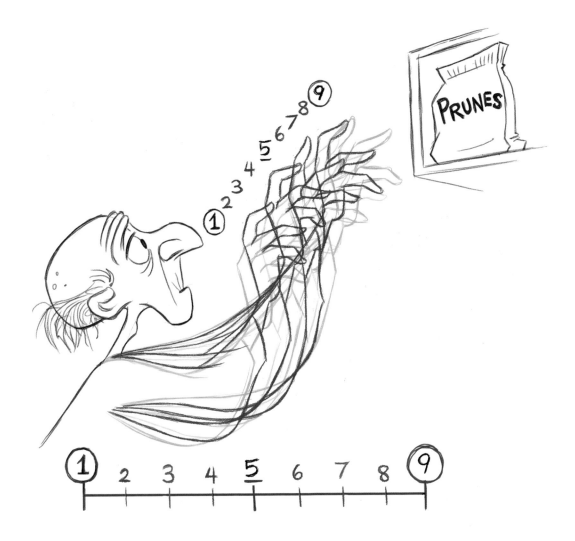

Incidentally, these drawings are spaced widely solely for the purpose of printed clarity. The technique looks best with slow timing, with the drawings close together, so the trembling parts really read.

"Thwacks" and stars – Used when a character crashes into something for cartoony impact, sometimes seen in conjunction with camera-shake.

Usually seen as a solidly painted effect, most often white, whose middle gets larger as it animates outward from impact and breaks up. Sometimes followed by stars that also animate outward and break up. Best ones are fast, on ones, and last long enough to cause a flash but not enough to overtake the action. Again, Irv Spence's Tom and Jerry ones are great, but are sometimes overused. (You don't need a thwack every time a character "takes" or lands softly!)

Dust clouds after a zip should animate backward from the thrust of movement, dissipate more slowly than they appear, and never break up in regular patterns.

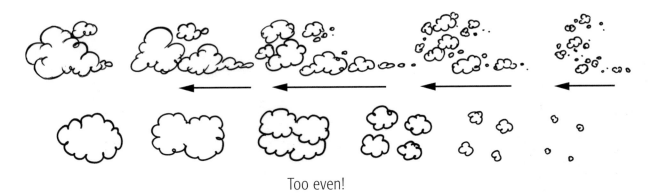

Too even!

Dust when something hits the ground should go outward from impact but can also rise upward when dissipating.

Vibrations can usually be executed one of three simple ways.

Method #1: Establish your settled position ㉑ and your widest swing points ①
and ②. Inbetween inward to the settled drawing (cushioning in) from each widest
swing point; one group on odd numbers, the other on even numbers.

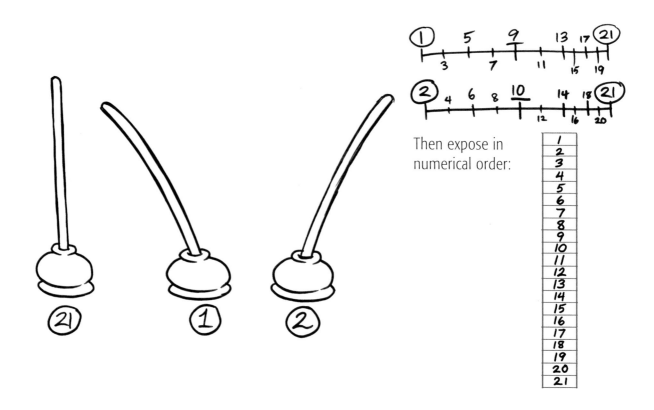

Then expose in
numerical order:

1
2
3
4
5
6
7
8
9
10
11
12
13
14
15
16
17
18
19
20
21

Method #2: Draw a key that superimposes *both* swing points in one drawing ① and inbetween inward (odd #'s) to the settled drawing ㉑.

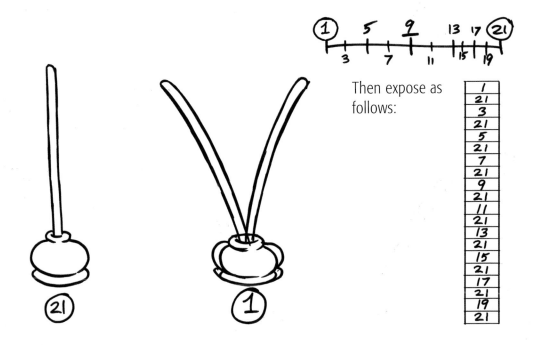

Then expose as follows:

1
21
3
21
5
21
7
21
9
21
11
21
13
21
15
21
17
21
19
21

Method #3: Exactly as Method #2, except your swing key is a multiple or smear that covers the entire area. Inbetween and expose as in Method #2.

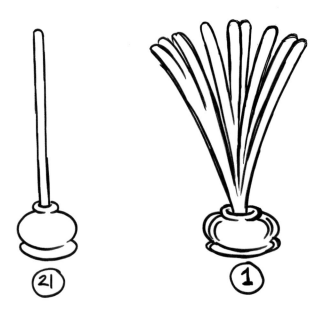

A nice variation on the vibration formula is the "double-path" method, often used while a character is progressing in movement:

Plan one set of keys (in this case, a shocked cat moving backward) and time on twos:

G 2

Then superimpose over the same path a second set of keys on the same timing but with even numbers.

Then expose:

1
2
3
4
5
6
7
8
9
10
11
12
13
14
15
16
17
18
19
20
21
22
23
24
25
26

Your animation will vibrate between the two positions while moving directionally. Check out Ward Kimball's shocked Ivan the Cat in *Peter and The Wolf*.

All of these methods work, and all should be on ones. Vibrations rarely look good on twos, but if you do, give plenty of looseness and drag where you can.

Staggers are used to convey strain, hesitance, skidding to a halt — in short, a staccato movement that constantly progresses to a peak or rest. An easy method is to establish your two keys and a timing chart on twos (usually best as a fairly constant rate).

G3

Expose first on twos:

1	
3	
5	
7	
9	
11	
13	
15	
17	
19	
21	
23	
25	
27	
29	
31	
33	
35	
37	

Then expose the ones (the same run of twos, but offset):

1	
5	
3	
7	
5	
9	
7	
11	
9	
13	
11	
15	
13	
17	
15	
19	
17	
21	
19	
23	
21	
25	
23	
27	
25	
29	
27	
31	
29	
33	
31	
35	
33	
37	
35	
37	
35	
37	

Note end exposure for a graceful finish

This type of movement again should almost always be on ones.

"Smear" (or elongated) and "multiple" drawings:

These drawings are often a more eye-pleasing substitute for blur lines, as they work more like a live-action blur by distorting the areas of broad color quickly enough for the eye not to detect a specific "effect." They're also good for time-compression as they can be used to get from one area to a completely different one in about three frames! If you want to see the great textbook examples of smear drawings (and this is how I learned about them), do some single-framing on the Chuck Jones classics *Wackiki Wabbit*, *The Dover Boys*, *Long-Haired Hare* (Lloyd Vaughn's animation of Bugs conducting), and *Case of the Missing Hare*, and the Bob Clampett masterpiece *A Corny Concerto* (the "Blue Danube" section, where Mama Swan is frantically looking in vain for her captured kiddies).

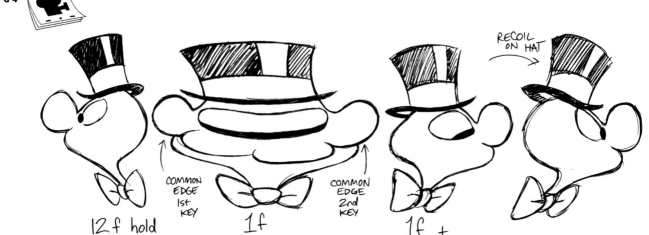

Basically, establish your two keys and draw your "smear" to wipe across, covering the farthest left and right points of both key drawings "in sync." The following drawings then fold into the key you're progressing into. Geez, who woulda thought a smear could be so technical?

G5

12f hold   1f   1f   into tiptoe action!

As above, a smear can be used to trigger an attitude change, and also continue into an action immediately (rather than stopping on the next key before continuing the movement). Note, too, that neither example has any anticipation before the smear. While much of the humor of a smear comes from its very abruptness, does this mean you can't precede it with a little anticipation? Of course not! Can you animate a little recoil after the smear? Certainly! Go with what feels best in the context of your film and your characters.

Smear effects should almost never be on twos, as then they are slow enough to be perceived as goony drawings by an audience! The same principles apply to "multiple" drawings:

G 6

12f hold   1f   1f + usually one more inbetween   12f hold

The only thing wrong with using "multiples" is that they are by nature more detailed than "smears," so they are a bit more readable as "effects" to an audience. (In fact, Chuck Jones makes a gag out of its obviousness in the opening to *Zipping Along*, where he freeze-frames on the most exaggerated multiple to superimpose the Coyote's Latin name underneath!)

One nice variation on the multiple is a "double-speed" inbetween – i.e., by multiplying the moving arm, hand, etc., it appears to progress to a midpoint and a *farther* point at the same time:

G 7

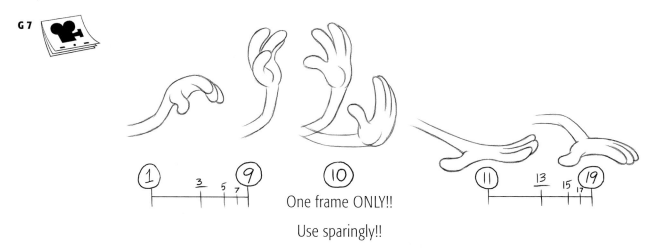

One frame ONLY!!

Use sparingly!!

There's a great scene of Madam Mim (Milt Kahl, I think) in *Sword and the Stone*, where she whirls her arm around in a circle, and for one frame has two arms. It plays great at speed, and – like all well-handled gimmicks – you never perceive the bizarre drawing at 24 fps.

Impact distortions: Not to be confused with a squash and recoil, this is a drawing that distorts much farther than the squash, for one frame only, which you *feel* rather than see. By using it for one frame only, it is not perceived as a distortion, but if you inbetween out of it, your character becomes too squashy-looking!

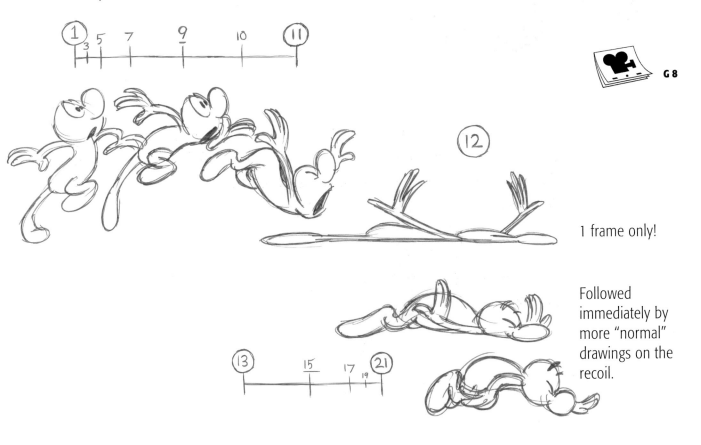

G 8

1 frame only!

Followed immediately by more "normal" drawings on the recoil.

A great example (and the one that inspired the above drawings) is from *101 Dalmatians*, where Roger body tackles the overeager Pongo in the park. Although this scene actually takes six frames to register the squash (three drawings on twos, to emphasize Pongo momentarily having the wind knocked out of him), the most extreme squash drawing is immediately followed by a normal one, giving the same kind of "pop back" to call attention to the contact.

This same principle applies to solid objects: By making it snap back immediately, the object's contact is felt without making it appear rubbery.

1f only!

This metal ball retains its shape for every drawing to reinforce its density, except for the one-frame contact to make its weight felt. My all-time favorite example of this idea is in Disney's *Peter Pan*: Captain Hook is about to bring his sword smashing down on top of Peter, who puts his arms up to resist. At the moment of impact, for one frame only, Peter Pan is drawn like this:

Seeing is believing!

Throwing a punch: Art Babbitt's approach to get the most impact and thrust out of a punch was not to show the actual contact! Rather, establish the victim's head position and show the assailant's arm progressing quickly toward it. *Then* show the fist past where the head was on the previous drawing and displace the head out of the way.

This is sometimes accompanied by a "white frame," in which the characters remain normal but the BG is replaced for one frame by white. I have to admit, there are also plenty of fine animated punches that do show the contact (my favorite: the one that comes out of the phone receiver in the Daffy/Elmer *A Pest in the House*).

Snapping into keys and freezes:

Sometimes you need no inbetweens at all to move from one pose to another if you prepare or recoil properly for it.

BANG! 16f hold!

(See Ben Washam's great Bugs takes in *Rabbit of Seville*.!)

G 9

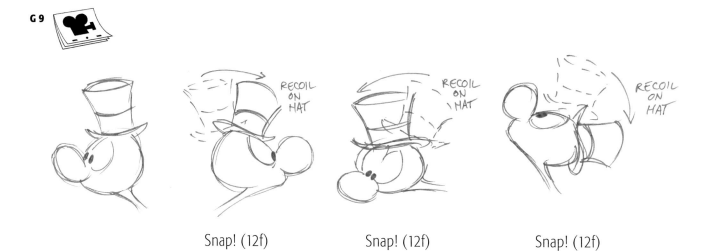

Snap! (12f)   Snap! (12f)   Snap! (12f)

(Inspired by the jailbird Wolf caught in the searchlight in Tex Avery's *Dumb-Hounded*…)

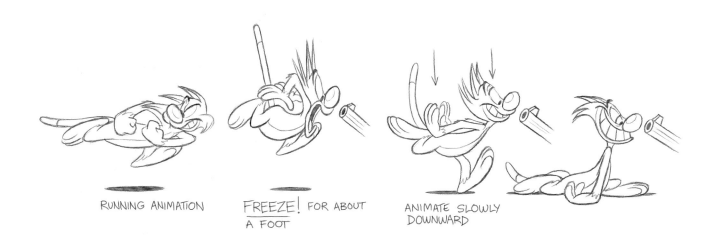

RUNNING ANIMATION   FREEZE! FOR ABOUT A FOOT   ANIMATE SLOWLY DOWNWARD

(Also see Bugs freezing to a midair stop in *Bugs Bunny Rides Again.*!)

Camera shakes: If your impact is vertical, plan a vertical shake; if it's horizontal, plan a horizontal one. Work outward from the center on your field guide and plan evenly spaced increments from either end (with maybe a cushion closest to the center). Letter or number alternating up, down, up, down.

Then expose on ones in the camera instructions column on the X–sheet:

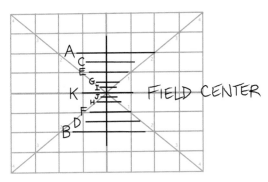

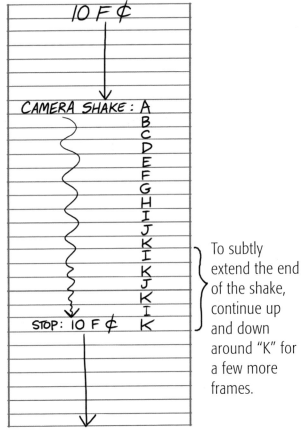

In this detail, position K is 10F¢.

To subtly extend the end of the shake, continue up and down around "K" for a few more frames.

Basically, it's the same principle as animating toward the center of a vibration, except you're doing it with the camera. In the illustration above, the camera shake spans from 2 fields North to 2 fields South on a 12-field grid center, meaning that the maximum field size allowable would be a 10 field. In other words, when the camera is at position A, the field will be at the top of the 12-field grid – any larger than a 10 field and you'd run out of artwork.

You can also "animate" a camera shake by throwing the fields off center and going in-out with the camera, as well as tilting the angles as you work toward the normal framing. Just remember, the smaller your field size (the dotted-line one, for example) the larger all the elements will appear on screen. Likewise, for a horizontal camera shake, if your first frame of the shake is to the left, your characters will appear on screen to be thrown to the right. (Hanna and Barbera use this idea to great effect when the cats slam into a Dutch door in *Saturday Evening Puss.*!)

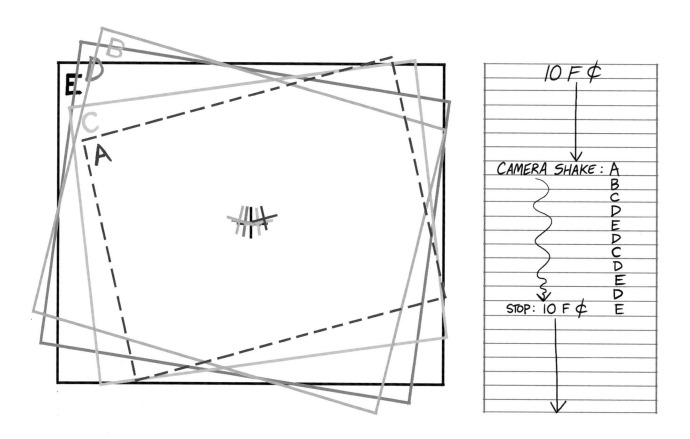

PUTTING IT ALL TOGETHER

Approach to a Scene

There has been a lot of information crammed into the preceding chapters, so in an effort to make some sense out of it, I humbly offer the way I would approach animating a traditional hand-drawn scene. Of course, this is merely one person's way – ask a million different animators, and they'll give you a million different ways – all valid!

Before you animate, review your knowledge of the characters

- What makes your character *who* he is? How does he look at life? What are his basic attitudes? How can you expand his range to acquire greater depth? How does he walk? Run? Rest? How can you show what he is thinking and feeling through his movements?

- How does your character interact with the other characters in the show? How does he compare and contrast with them? What properties of drawing and movement make your character unique to the others around him?

- How *old* is your character? What is his weight and mass, and how does that affect his movement? How physically fit is your character? How weak?
  What are the ground rules for your character that you should never, ever, ever break? When should you break them?

Approach to a scene

- ### Get briefed

  - **The Director** will tell you the big-picture stuff – the context of the scene within the sequence, how it cuts with scenes around it, and the main story points and acting beats you need to communicate.

  - **The Supervising Animator** (or **Animation Director**) will tell you the details and specifics – *how* does your character perform in this scene? What should be the primary action of the scene and what should be secondary? Are there specific timing ideas the supervisor would like to see in the scene?

  - **Go back to the original storyboards** – Don't just look at the layouts you're given in the scene folder – as layout artists are primarily concerned with the staging and size relationships of the characters. Often, the original boards will contain more acting information, even if they haven't been "cinematically" conceived. If you can access the cut story reels, with production dialogue cut and timed to the boards, even better.

- ### Listen to the soundtrack

  - Study the performance enough times to commit it to memory (highs, lows, attitude changes, hard accents, etc.). If possible, you should be able to do a creditable delivery of the performance itself. Continue referring to the track during animation, but you should feel familiar enough with it to hit your main accents correctly.

■ Number and pre-time your X-sheets

- Number the whole scene on odd #'s (1, 3, 5, 7) on twos. This gives you a road map to see where certain accents hit certain frame #'s. Single inbetweens can be put in later as even #'s.
- Pre-time your sheets, establishing rhythms and pauses.

After a while, pre-timing will give you a very clear indication of the textures and variations in the scene. Especially helpful for rhythmic actions such as walking, running, hammering, swimming, etc. Because your sheets are pre-numbered, you'll be able to establish numerically where certain actions might fall.

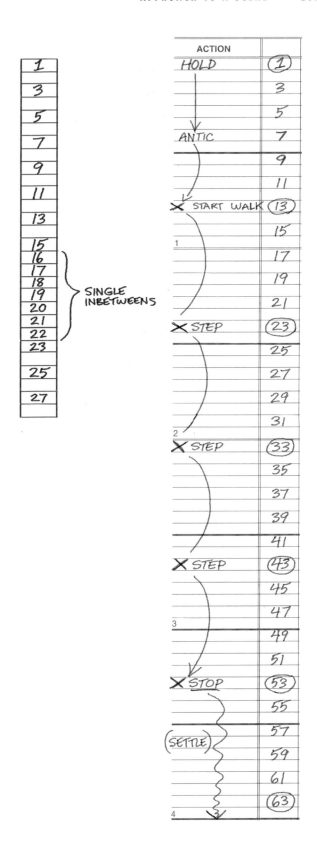

■ Okay, now you can draw

- **To thumbnail or not to thumbnail?** Many animators find this a useful and valuable part of the process – perfectly valid. I tend *not* to thumbnail when animating, since I prefer drawing on the large page and seeing the drawings relate to one another in a pile I can flip. I thumbnail a lot prior to storyboarding, which, of course, incorporates a lot of "animation thinking." The choice is yours.

- **Establish your storytelling drawings:**
  - Think like a comic-strip artist, establishing attitude poses (and don't forget to use the spine!). The great comic artists had the ability to encapsulate an attitude and action in a single pose. The more you think like this, the easier it is to add the animation bells and whistles later. Don't worry about timing at this stage – just succinct communication.

  - Your initial storytelling drawings are not necessarily the broadest extremes in your action. Rather, they are the ones most comfortable for the audience to settle on to "tell the story" of the scene. The "Name That Tune" school of animation ("I can name that scene in five drawings, Bill!"): if you can tell the story of the scene concisely, in just a few drawings that communicate, you have done the bulk of the scene's work. I recommend working lightly at this stage, to allow for more refinement and flow as you draw when tying down later.

  - *Finding* those elusive poses – do your drawings answer these criteria?
    - *What communicates best?*
    - *What communicates best and is unexpected?*
      I throw out a lot of roughs when trying to find the right pose. Being able to communicate the ideas of the character's emotions is what I consider fulfilling the basic requirement. It takes more investigating (and self-criticism) to arrive at drawings that communicate but are interesting, unexpected, and unique to the character.

  - Alternatively, animate your keys lightly in a straight-ahead manner, for further refinement when you tie them down later.

  - Phrasing – Listen to the "musical line" of the dialogue and draw to reflect it. Think of *one* interesting pattern to reflect a sentence, instead of hitting random accents indiscriminately.

- Place your key drawings on the X-sheets to your pre-timed numbers:
  - Use your best guess, based on intuition and how long you want certain expressions to read.
  - Once you can relate drawings to numbers, you can see how many frames land between your keys and start charting your timing.
  - The charts should not imply that all that is left are dead-in-the-middle inbetweens. (Just because you might chart a BD to fall directly in the middle doesn't mean it should be drawn that way.) Use the charts as rough guides for spacing (and the order in which the BDs and inbetweens should be drawn), but add the bells-and-whistles animation stuff in the next stages.
- Start adding the breakdowns:
  - Use them to add the "juice" to your action, fleshing out, developing arcs, adding overlap, going beyond, and recoiling.
  - Drawing a breakdown with parts on different timings and spacing adds interest to your work with a minimum of extra effort. (If you do it more with *drawing* than with separate charts for every appendage and eyeblink, it will keep the figure more organically unified.)
- Tie down your keys and breakdowns:
  - I usually like to do this straight-ahead from start to finish, as it gives a more organic relationship to the flow of the drawings.
  - Go back in and add all the partials, eccentric actions, and lip-sync — anything you need to give your animation the subtle "grace notes" that will make it alive. If you have the luxury of a rough inbetweener following you up, leave anything that will be a dead-in-the-middle inbetween (slow-moving torsos, craniums, hard objects).
- Add final inbetweens (rough):
  - At this point, all that should be left are easily subdividable inbetweens (½'s, ¼'s, ⅛'s), usually done by the rough inbetweener in a separate color (most often blue). That way, when the scene goes to clean-up, the artists can automatically see which drawings are important, done by the animator, and which have been added by the rough inbetweener to complete the actions. On a

"partial," it will differentiate between the eccentric part drawn by the animator, and the rest of the drawing that would be a dead-in-the-middle inbetween.

■ Lest you think this pose-to-pose approach won't always work in every situation — you're right! Sometimes just good ol' straight-ahead is the only way that'll work. Use your judgment!

So, in a nutshell:

■ **Review your character's qualities.**

■ **Get briefed.**

■ **Listen to the soundtrack.**

■ **Pre-time and number your X-sheets on twos.**

■ **Draw your storytelling poses.**

■ **Place the keys on your X-sheets.**

■ **Chart your timing on the keys.**

■ **Draw the breakdowns.**

■ **Tie down the keys and breakdowns in a straight-ahead fashion.**

■ **Go back in and draw the inbetweens and partials.**

22

Things for Animators to Do to Make Their Lives (and Everyone Else's) Easier!

- Circle your keys **㉑** and underline your breakdowns **25**. It will help clean-up quickly identify all the important drawings.

- Color-code your animation:

  Black – all key poses, breakdowns, eccentric actions, and partials

  Blue – someone else's rough inbetweens

  Red – tracebacks, with the indication ⑱ G-25 also in red.

It is the industry standard, created at Disney, used for generations. It is a sure-fire way to guarantee everything you want is reflected in the clean-up.

- When animating on twos, use *odd* numbers only: 1, 3, 5, 7, etc. That way, when you add singles, you can use even numbers for the inbetweens, and your numbering is still accurate to the scene's frame count.
- When charting your drawings:
  - put them on the corresponding drawing number to the beginning of the chart:

 belongs on Drawing 15, not Drawing 23

  - circle your keys and underline breakdowns on your charts as well as the drawings.
  - Don't chart inbetweens on *thirds*:

It's always more accurate to chart on multiples of ½'s, ¼'s, ⅛'s because the inbetweens can fall directly in the middle with no guesswork.

If you chart like this: your breakdown on 5 can be an eccentric drawing that would essentially accomplish the same thing when inbetween 3 is put in. If you must use thirds, draw one of the inbetweens yourself so the remaining one can be subdivided evenly.

  - Don't space inbetweens so closely together that you can't fit a drawing in:

This chart for a moving hold (known in the industry as "railroad tracks") might boil and look very even and dull.

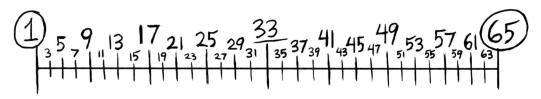

You might be better served by a chart with half the drawings that cushions in to a *hold* for 27-65, with an occasional blink to break it up.

■ Don't expose contacting characters out of phase by a frame. It will be impossible for them to interact correctly, and doubly impossible to clean up.

FINKY RENFREW

F-1	R-1
	2
3	
	4
5	
	6
7	
	8
9	
	10
11	
	12
13	
	14
15	
	16
F-17	
	R-18

Also, when animating a second character in contact with a first character already completed, try to use the same numbering if possible — it helps all involved with the scene to maintain proper registration between the levels.

■ Don't chart tiny moving holds on ones! Twos should be fine, even during trucks and pans if the drawings are close together enough.

23

Is That All, Folks?

That's intended to be a rhetorical question, really, although the medium of animation has certainly had a roller-coaster ride in recent years. While it's true to say that interest in the medium is still high, economics, audience tastes, and studio politics have all contributed to the early death knells for hand-drawn animation, as well as the rampant bandwagonism of assuming that if it's rendered in CG, it's a hit. We all know that neither scenario is true, but that's primarily due to the fact that the people who really love the art form are the ones keeping it alive, in any technique that works, as long as the results are great stories and great characters. I first got into this business in the 1970's, when Disney was out of fashion and people were already proclaiming the medium dead, save for Saturday Morning TV. It didn't matter – I knew it was what I loved and how I wanted to spend my artistic life, and who cared what the naysayers thought, anyway? I was fortunate enough in my formative years to meet enough like-minded people to convince me that if I was crazy, at least there are several others with me in the loony wagon.

Well, I'm still here, and so is Disney, and so are a plethora of studios and independent filmmakers who say it's not over yet. I dedicate this last word to the students and future animators who also say it's not over yet, and hope this book helps them, just a little, to realize their true animation potential.

About the Author

Eric Goldberg is a veteran Director, Designer, and Animator who has worked extensively in New York, London, and Hollywood, creating feature films, commercials, title sequences, and television specials. He is equally at home with traditional hand-drawn animation and the most up-to-date computer animation, and has pioneered groundbreaking techniques in both worlds.

Eric's animation knowledge started early, creating flip books at age six and eventually making Super-8 films from the age of 13. His teenage years included guest appearances on local Philadelphia television programs, as well as a national appearance on *To Tell the Truth*. Eric's Super-8 films won top prizes in the Kodak Teenage Movie Awards, including 1974's Grand Prize for summer film courses at the University of Southern California.

Eric received a full scholarship to Pratt Institute in Brooklyn, New York, where he majored in Illustration, and took supplemental animation and film courses.

His first professional jobs were free-lance animation while still in school (including one from his animation teacher!), and he eventually wound up as a full-time assistant animator on *Raggedy Ann & Andy*, directed by Richard Williams in New York City. There, he worked with master animator Tissa David (UPA, Hubley Studios) as well as animation legends Emery Hawkins (Walter Lantz, Warner Bros., Hubley Studios) and Art Babbitt (Disney, UPA, Hubley, Quartet).

When the film was completed, Richard Williams invited Eric to work in his London studio as a director-animator on countless television spots. He had the good fortune to work with Ken Harris at that time, learning techniques honed during Ken's stint as Chuck Jones' greatest animator (Bugs Bunny, Daffy Duck, Road Runner, Pepé Le Pew, et al.). Eric's association with Richard Williams continued in Los Angeles, where Eric served as Director of Animation on the Emmy-winning "Ziggy's Gift," based on the popular newspaper cartoon.

Eric met his future wife, Susan, while on holiday in New York, where she was the head background painter for Zander's Animation Parlour. Married during the making of "Ziggy," Eric and Susan have enjoyed both a personal and professional relationship, with Susan frequently serving as Art Director on their projects together. The two of them landed back in London, where Eric co-founded Pizazz Pictures. At this commercials studio with a worldwide clientele, he directed spots with such diverse techniques as cel-animation, brush-painting, stop-motion and pixillation, colored-pencil rendering, live-action and animation combinations, and digital compositing.

Eventually, after the success of films like *Who Framed Roger Rabbit?* and *The Little Mermaid*, Disney came knocking at Eric's door, and convinced him to return to California for what turned out to be a 10-year run at the studio.

Eric's first assignment was as Supervising Animator of *Aladdin*'s wise-cracking Genie, who endlessly morphed and shape-shifted into whatever form the brilliant mind of Robin Williams could conjure up. After that, he co-directed the successful *Pocahontas*, the first Disney feature based on events and people who actually existed as a vivid part of America's history.

Eric then animated the feisty Danny DeVito-voiced satyr Phil in *Hercules*, and followed that with a stint on *Fantasia/2000*. Eric directed, wrote, and animated two critically acclaimed sequences for that film: "Carnival of the Animals" (flamingos with yo-yos, rendered in animated watercolor) and "Rhapsody in Blue," a slice-of-life story of intersecting lives, set in 1930's New York. The piece, a labor of love, was inspired by both George Gershwin and the legendary theatrical caricaturist Al Hirschfeld, who served as Artistic Consultant. Susan brought her formidable talents to the film as Art Director on both sequences.

Also during his time at Disney, Eric experimented with ground-breaking computer-animation techniques, which replicated the fluidity and "squash and stretch" of the best hand-drawn animation — first on a Roger Rabbit test sequence, and then on the Tokyo Disney Seas theme-park attraction "Magic Lamp Theatre," starring Eric's signature character, the Genie, in stereoscopic, gratuitously-throw-everything-at-the-audience, 3-D computer animation.

Eric spent a year at Universal Studios developing Maurice Sendak's *Where the Wild Things Are* as a CG-animated feature film, until the project became bogged down in classic "development hell." From there, he went across the street to Warner Bros., becoming Animation Director on the live-action/animation feature *Looney Tunes: Back in Action*, directed by Joe Dante. Joe and Eric considered their work on the film a personal tribute to the late Chuck Jones, who was friend to both and peerless among his colleagues as the most brilliant animation director ever at Warner Bros. On this film, Eric got to handle the legendary Bugs, Daffy, Elmer, Wile E. Coyote, Yosemite Sam and the entire Warners stable, as well as provide the voices (!) for Speedy Gonzales, Tweety, and Marvin the Martian.

Recently Eric directed a 12-minute high-definition cartoon for a Buddhist cultural center in Hong Kong. "A Monkey's Tale" is the fanciful story of three monkeys who attempt to steal a peach from the hand of the ancient Monkey King, and learn a lesson in greed in the bargain. Also recently completed is Eric's direction of 4 minutes of brand-new animation starring Disney's "The Three Caballeros" (Donald Duck, José Carioca, and Panchito) for the updated Mexico Pavilion at EPCOT Center in Florida.

At present, Eric is back at his alma mater, Walt Disney Animation Studios, serving as Supervising Animator for "Louis" (the trumpet-playing alligator) in Disney's upcoming hand-drawn animated feature *The Princess and the Frog*, slated for a holiday 2009 release.